Blender 3D 2.49
Incredible Machines

Modeling, rendering, and animating realistic machines
with Blender 3D

Allan Brito

BIRMINGHAM - MUMBAI

Blender 3D 2.49 Incredible Machines

First published: November 2009

Production Reference: 1121109

Published by Packt Publishing Ltd.
32 Lincoln Road
Olton
Birmingham, B27 6PA, UK.

ISBN 978-1-847197-46-7

www.packtpub.com

Cover Image by Vinayak Chittar (vinayak.chittar@gmail.com)

Credits

Author
Allan Brito

Reviewers
Claudio "malefico" Andaur

Yorik van Havre

Acquisition Editor
David Barnes

Development Editor
Swapna V. Verlekar

Technical Editor
Aanchal Kumar

Indexer
Rekha Nair

Editorial Team Leader
Gagandeep Singh

Project Team Leader
Lata Basantani

Project Coordinator
Joel Goveya

Proofreader
Jade Schuler

Production Coordinator
Aparna Bhagat

Cover Work
Aparna Bhagat

About the Author

Allan Brito is a Brazilian architect specialized in information visualization. He lives and works in Recife, Brazil. He works with Blender 3D to produce animations and still images for visualization and instructional material. Besides his work with Blender as an artist, he also has a large experience in teaching and researching about 3D modeling, animation, and multimedia.

He is an active member of the community of Blender users, writing about Blender 3D and its development for websites in Brazilian Portuguese (http://www.allanbrito.com) and English (http://www.blendernation.com).

This is his third book on Blender 3D, the first one was *Blender 3D – Guia do Usuário*, which was published in Brazil. It's a guide on how to use Blender that covers everything from the basics to character animation. The second book, *Blender 3D: Architecture, Buildings, and Scenery*, covers the use of Blender for architectural visualization. It is written in English, and is published by Packt Publishing.

He can be reached at his website, http://www.blender3darchitect.com, where he covers the use of Blender 3D and other tools for architectural visualization.

I would like to thank my family for supporting me during the production of this book, especially my wife Érica, and my parents Maria and Luiz.

About the Reviewers

Claudio "malefico" Andaur is an argentine CG artist residing in Buenos Aires. He graduated as a Chemical Engineer from Universidad Tecnologica Nacional, Buenos Aires, Argentina in 1998.

He started working with Blender and open source applications in 2000. He was increasingly involved in Blender animation projects mainly for television shows. In 2003, he was part of the team who wrote the *Blender 2.3 Official Guide*. In 2005, he quit his regular job as an engineer and started working as one of the project leaders of *Plumiferos*, a CG feature film project made in Blender. In his blog (www.malefico3d.org), he likes to write about character animation, rigging, and personal projects. In 2008, he started his own animation studio called **Licuadora Studio** (www.licuadorastudio.com).

Claudio, better known as "malefico" in the Blender community, has given lectures and classes in Argentina, Venezuela, Colombia, Belgium, and Spain, as well as the Blender Conference in Amsterdam, The Netherlands on several occasions.

> I'd like to thank my wife Laura for her constant support and patience, and my fellow Licuadores: Ivan, Manuel, and Diego.

Yorik van Havre is a Belgian architect who currently lives and works in Brazil. Blender occupies a big portion of his daily work. He regularly writes articles and tutorials about Blender, architecture, and architecture software, and is actively involved in several communities and open source projects. He has also reviewed Allan's previous book, *Blender 3D: Architecture, Buildings, and Scenery*. More about Yorik's work can be found at his website: http://yorik.orgfree.com.

Table of Contents

Preface

Blender 3D provides all the features that you need for creating super-realistic 3D models of machines for use in artwork, movies, and computer games. *Blender 3D 2.49 Incredible Machines* gives you step-by-step instructions for building weapons, vehicles, robots, and more.

This book will show you how to use Blender 3D for mechanical modeling and product visualization. Through the pages of the book, you will find a step-by-step guide to create three different projects: a fantasy weapon, a spacecraft, and a giant robot. Even though these machines are not realistic, you will be able to build your own sensible and incredible machines with the techniques that you will learn in this book along with the exercises and examples.

All three sections of this book, which cover three projects, are planned to have an increasing learning curve. The first project is about a hand weapon, where we will model a small-sized object with tiny details. This first part of the book will show you how to deal with these details and model them in Blender 3D.

In the second project, we will create a spacecraft, adding a bit of scale to the project, as well as new materials and textures. With this project, we will be working with metal, glass, and other elements that make the spacecraft.

At the end, we have a big and complex object, which is a transforming robot. This last part of the book will cover the modeling of two objects and show how you can make one transform into the other. The scale and number of objects in this project are quite big, but the same principles, as in the other projects, are applied here with a step-by-step guide on how to go through the workflow of the project.

What this book covers

Chapter 1: Machinery Modeling and Visualization with Blender introduces us to a few concepts and relevant information about this book and, of course, talks a bit about this incredible software called Blender 3D, and how we can take advantage of all of the tools of Blender. It gives a brief description of its history and also explains us the concept of an Incredible Machine.

Chapter 2: Modeling a Handgun gets us started with working on the first of the three projects of this book—modeling of a handgun. It explains why a handgun was chosen for our first project, what the final image of the project will look like, our modeling workflow, and the modeling technique that will be used to work on this project.

Chapter 3: Polygon Modeling of the Weapon guides you through the first steps of the modeling by using concept drawings to create a base model in Blender. The base model is very important to add details and upgrade the first flat surfaces into something more complex. This chapter tells us how to set up and configure a background image, and how to model and transform a mesh by using the background image as a guide. It also demonstrates the use of various tools such as Edge Loop tool, Face Loop Cut tool, and 3D Cursor as a tool.

Chapter 4: Adding Details adds a few more details to the model created in the previous chapter. It teaches us to create creases, and use the new snapping tools and others such as the Spin tool and Bevel tool.

Chapter 5: Rendering the Project with YafaRay winds up the weapon project with the setup of textures and materials for the model, and the installation and setup of an external render engine for Blender 3D. The render engine for this project is YafaRay, which allows us to use advanced global illumination features not available in the Blender internal render. This chapter describes how to install and use the renderer to use it in more detail with the next project.

Chapter 6: Steampunk Spacecraft describes what steampunk is and what the characteristics of a steampunk machine are. It initializes the creation of a steampunk spacecraft with even smaller details and more UV Mapping techniques to add more realism to the model. It creates a base mesh for the spacecraft and also gives us an experience in edge modeling, deforming, and adjusting the shape of a model to get the shape of the desired object.

Chapter 7: Working with Smaller Areas adds more details and parts to the base model created in the previous chapter. It teaches us how to use the Spin tool to create rounded bevels, how to work with curves and the different curves of Blender, how to create cables and wires with curves, and how to twist curves.

Chapter 8: Advanced UV Mapping will teach us how to add a few extra details with textures, which can be a great help in any modeling project. One of the advantages of using a great set of textures to create details is the ability to use images instead of models to create geometry.

Chapter 9: Putting the Spacecraft to Fly and Shoot with Special Effects uses some special effects to put our spacecraft in outer space and even make both weapons shoot! All these effects are created with a mix of particles and materials that generate the effects in a very short time. Both techniques and tools help a lot in this project, and can be used in other 3D modeling and rendering projects as well. It adds even more elements and visual aids to our project in order to bring more realism to the scene.

Chapter 10: Rendering the Spacecraft with YafaRay teaches us a bit more about YafaRay and renders our spacecraft project with it to achieve a photo-real effect from the lighting and materials. It demonstrates the spacecraft flying at both daylight and night environments. Along with the rendering process of YafaRay, it also teaches how to set up the environment settings, render methods, and materials of YafaRay.

Chapter 11: Transforming Robot initializes the work on the last Incredible Machine—a transforming robot. It is the most complex and difficult project of the three and, as you can imagine, it is about a robot that can transform its shape into something else. This chapter creates the base model of the robot, and tells us the differences between poly and subdivision modeling. It also describes what LuxRender is.

Chapter 12: Using Modifiers and Curves to Create Details for the Robot and Scene continues the modeling process by using some modifiers and curves turned into 3D meshes in order to add more details to the overall model. Along with the robot, its starts the creation of the scenario used to create the robot in LuxRender, using a few tricks and special materials to give it sci-fi look. It teaches us how to work with the bevel, array, and simple deform modifiers and how to deform curves by using hooks.

Chapter 13: Making the Robot Look Metallic with Materials in LuxRender assembles all parts into the robot model and adds materials to the model in LuxRender. This chapter teaches us how to install LuxRender and export our scenes to the renderer, how to set up the basic parameters of LuxRender materials, how to choose from several preset materials of LuxRender, and how to add textures to 3D models in order for LuxRender to recognize the material.

Chapter 14: Adding Lights to the Scene and Rendering with LuxRender is the next step in the creation of our third Incredible Machine project. It explains us the working of lights and effects, and makes the light interact with the materials and textures to give reflections and other optical effects that result in a very nice illumination effect. Besides the setting up lights in LuxRender, it also adds lots of elements and creates the scenario to receive the robot model in the next chapter.

Chapter 15: It's Alive! Animating the Robot assembles our robot and uses animation tools to create the transforming movement of the machine. By using the same controls, we can easily create animations with Blender and render the movement in LuxRender.

Chapter 16: Post-production of the Robot takes us through the post-production process of the robot in LuxRender that can be executed at the renderer window. It shows us how to make the necessary adjustments to the image inside LuxRender. It teaches us to add lens effects in the rendering to make the image look like a photograph, add color schemes to fit artificial and natural lighting, remove the noise of the image with LuxRender.

What you need for this book

The Blender Foundation recommends the following minimum requirements:

- Three-button mouse
- Open GL Graphics Card with 16 MB RAM
- 300 MHz CPU
- 128 MB RAM
- 1024 x 768 pixels display with 16-bit color
- 20 MB free hard disk space

However, if you really want to get maximum performance, there is a more powerful configuration:

- Three-button mouse
- Open GL Graphics Card with 128 or 256 MB RAM
- 2 GHz dual core CPU
- 2 GB RAM
- 1920 x 1200 pixels display with 24-bit color

There isn't much to say about the software, only that you can run Blender on almost any operating system available. The following is the list of systems that support Blender:

- Windows 98, ME, 2000, XP, or Vista
- Mac OS X 10.2 and later
- Linux i386, x86_64/amd64 or PPC
- FreeBSD 6.2 i386 and later
- Irix 6.5 mips3
- Solaris 2.8 sparc

Who this book is for

This book targets game designers/developers, artists, and product designers who want to create realistic images, 3D models, and videos of machines. The book will also help Blender artists interested in external renders like YafaRay and LuxRender, to add more realism to their projects. No previous experience of working with Blender 3D, YafaRay or LuxRender is required.

Conventions

In this book, you will find a number of styles of text that distinguish between different kinds of information. Here are some examples of these styles, and an explanation of their meaning.

New terms and **important words** are shown in bold. Words that you see on the screen, in menus or dialog boxes for example, appear in the text like this: "Go to the **Edit** panel and locate the **BevOb** option, which is located right below the menu ".

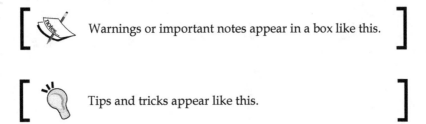

Warnings or important notes appear in a box like this.

Tips and tricks appear like this.

Reader feedback

Feedback from our readers is always welcome. Let us know what you think about this book—what you liked or may have disliked. Reader feedback is important for us to develop titles that you really get the most out of.

To send us general feedback, simply send an email to feedback@packtpub.com, and mention the book title via the subject of your message.

If there is a book that you need and would like to see us publish, please send us a note in the **SUGGEST A TITLE** form on www.packtpub.com or email suggest@packtpub.com.

If there is a topic that you have expertise in and you are interested in either writing or contributing to a book on, see our author guide on www.packtpub.com/authors.

Customer support

Now that you are the proud owner of a Packt book, we have a number of things to help you to get the most from your purchase.

Errata

Although we have taken every care to ensure the accuracy of our content, mistakes do happen. If you find a mistake in one of our books—maybe a mistake in the text or the code—we would be grateful if you would report this to us. By doing so, you can save other readers from frustration, and help us to improve subsequent versions of this book. If you find any errata, please report them by visiting http://www.packtpub.com/support, selecting your book, clicking on the **let us know** link, and entering the details of your errata. Once your errata are verified, your submission will be accepted and the errata added to any list of existing errata. Any existing errata can be viewed by selecting your title from http://www.packtpub.com/support.

Piracy

Piracy of copyright material on the Internet is an ongoing problem across all media. At Packt, we take the protection of our copyright and licenses very seriously. If you come across any illegal copies of our works, in any form, on the Internet, please provide us with the location address or website name immediately so that we can pursue a remedy.

Please contact us at copyright@packtpub.com with a link to the suspected pirated material.

We appreciate your help in protecting our authors, and our ability to bring you valuable content.

Questions

You can contact us at questions@packtpub.com if you are having a problem with any aspect of the book, and we will do our best to address it.

1
Machinery Modeling and Visualization with Blender

Welcome to the first chapter of Blender 3D—Incredible Machines! This chapter will introduce you to a few concepts and relevant information about this book, and of course, talk a bit about this incredible software called Blender 3D and how we can take advantage of all of the tools of Blender.

Before we start talking about more technical stuff, such as modeling surfaces and polygons for our machines, let's just answer this simple question: *What is Blender 3D?* Blender 3D is a very powerful 3D graphics suite, which is open source and available for almost all of the operating systems in the market. One of its most impressive features is that it's light weight and can run on computers that don't have updated hardware.

Blender history

Blender is an open source software available for anyone to use and create 3D content, but it wasn't always like this. When Blender was created, the software was a proprietary platform developed by a Dutch studio called NeoGeo (not related to the NeoGeo game console) and a company called Not a Number (NaN). The primary creator and developer of Blender is Ton Roosendaal. He was involved in the technical development of Blender at NeoGeo and the marketing of NaN.

By 2002, the investors behind NaN decided to end all operations of the company, including the development of Blender 3D. In the same year, Ton Roosendaal created the **Blender Foundation** to promote the use and development of Blender as an open source project, using the GNU Public License (GPL). With the Free Blender worldwide campaign, the foundation was able to raise 100,000 EUR necessary to buy the source code from NaN and release Blender to the world.

Today, Ton Roosendaal runs the Blender Foundation and the newly established Blender Institute that organizes the development and promotion of Blender.

Working with Blender

Well, if you are planning to work on high-definition videos or complex models, you will need updated hardware. It's all a matter of scale; when we work on big projects with complex models and high-definition renderings, more will be required from both Blender 3D and the hardware. The good news is that, for most of the projects, these full resolution tools and complex models won't be required.

With Blender, we can work on projects that involve polygonal modeling, 3D animation, and setup textures. We can work on materials with nodes and even create interactive animations. This book won't deal with interactive animation features of Blender, but the rest of the tools will be used to work on our projects.

As Blender is an open source and free software, if you don't have it yet, visit the Blender Foundation website to download it (`http://www.blender.org`). You will be amazed by the size of the software, which is only about 20 MB. It's quite impressive for a software that can produce images and animations just like the tools such as 3Ds Max, Maya, and Softimage XSI can.

Blender 3D, YafaRay, and GIMP

This book was written when Blender 2.49a was the most updated version of the software, so throughout the book, the same version has been used for the images and examples. The previous versions of Blender brought forward a few important updates for any artist interested in working with mechanical modeling, such as snapping improvements that will make modeling with precision easier. The snapping tools are one of the examples of the tools that we will be using to improve our work, and this will probably be the first book dealing with those tools.

As you may already know, Blender development never stops, and right now, the Blender Foundation is working hard on the next version of Blender, which will be Blender 2.50. They are planning complete re-formulations of the Blender interface and tools. This book is organized and planned in a way that will allow you to follow the workflow of the projects, regardless of the Blender version you are using.

For all our projects, we will not only be using Blender 3D, but also a set of tools that will enable us to create some great images. Along with Blender 3D, we will use YafaRay and GIMP. The first one is the most-used external renderer that can add advanced global illumination options to the renders created in Blender 3D. What's the reason most-used using YafaRay? Blender is a powerful software for modeling and animation, but so far, it can only add more realism to images and renders by using a technique called **Ambient Occlusion**.

The YafRay render engine is well know by previous Blender users because it was the best and the only tool to render with global illumination for a long time. However, in the past few months, the YafRay core has been completely rewritten and has given birth to YafaRay, which is the most recent and updated version of the software. The name was changed from YafRay to YafaRay to reflect the changes in the render engine core. In this book, we will cover the tools and options to use YafaRay to render our images. The setup and workflow of the images will have to follow a few rules to work on YafaRay, but the final result will show the reward for our efforts. Just for the record, YafaRay is an open source project like Blender 3D, and you can find more information about it from its official website: http://www.yafaray.org.

Finally, GIMP is the best solution in the open source world to edit and create **texture maps** for 3D software. In all of our projects, we will have to create and edit images called texture maps. These texture maps have to be created or edited in some software (that even have the ability to edit and paint them) — Blender can't do everything alone. That's why we will use GIMP as a part of the workflow for our projects. The GIMP software can be downloaded from its official website: http://www.gimp.org.

What is an Incredible Machine?

Now that we know a bit more about Blender and the other tools that we will be using, let's talk about the main subject of the book, which is Incredible Machines! What is an Incredible Machine? Well, it's a kind of machine that doesn't exist in our world, has amazing capabilities, and has a great sci-fi look. One of its main characteristics is its element of fantasy related with its nature. Several books and movies, such as steampunk stories or sci-fi movies, often use machines that don't exist in our world.

When we start our projects in the next chapters, you'll notice that the best part about working on projects like this is that we don't have any boundaries that will hold down our imagination. In fact, after reading this book, you should design and create your own Incredible Machines! Just pick a machine that exists today, and turn it into something better, with stronger sources of energy and new tools.

Knowing the potential of these machines, we will work on three main projects that will deal with very different types of machines. Let's see how the book is organized.

How the book is organized

We now know that the book is about incredible mechanical models and vehicles with extreme designs, all modeled and created with Blender 3D. But, how will we be working on those models along the book? The entire book is organized into three big modeling projects, which will require skills in textures, effects, and animation.

For each project, an Incredible Machine has been chosen. The order in which those projects are placed creates a continuous learning curve, ranging from a simple project to a more complex and difficult one to finish. Here are the three projects that we will cover in the book:

1. **Part I**: Creating a handgun.
2. **Part II**: Modeling and rendering a steampunk spacecraft.
3. **Part III**: Modeling and animating a transforming robot.

As we can see, the first project is a smaller object on scale and will be the easiest of the three to accomplish. The last project will be the most complex one.

All of the projects have been designed with a **PBL (Project Based Learning)** approach, where you will follow the orientations of each project and learn a few tricks and workarounds with Blender tools to solve common modeling problems. The workflow for each project is based on real projects and follows the same structure that you would find in major studios, or with more experienced freelance artists.

Here is the basic workflow for all of the chapters:

1. Project concept and design.
2. Analysis of reference images and photos.
3. Plan and study the modeling.
4. Work with textures and materials.
5. Create and edit texture maps.
6. Export to YafaRay.
7. Render final images.
8. Post production of the images when needed.

We will follow this workflow for each project and add steps when necessary.

Do I have to know Blender already?

Here is an important aspect to consider! The answer for that question is, yes! This book won't cover basic Blender features, such as the interface or keyboard shortcut lists. The book has been planned for artists who already have a minimum knowledge of how Blender works, how to create simple models, and how to add materials, lights, and basic animations.

This doesn't mean that some tools or concepts won't be explained, but we will certainly skip the basics. However, some topics require a few extra explanations, even for more experienced users, such as the new tools added to Blender in the last updates, and of course, the integration between Blender 3D and YafaRay. This will be explained in the initial chapters about rendering, followed by some extra details in each project along the book.

The main goal of the book is to give tips and insights about modeling and rendering techniques in Blender, where you can take examples and projects in the book and apply different ideas to create a new incredible or standard machine. Knowing Blender 3D, or at least the basics, will be extremely important to start out quickly with the book. As stated before, the book won't cover the basics.

Before you begin your Incredible Machine projects, you should be familiar with the following:

- How the Blender interface works
- Opening and managing windows
- Managing and changing working modes
- Setting up basic materials
- Adding basic lights to a scene
- Managing and adding cameras to scenes

Working with mesh objects is not difficult, but with these basic aspects of Blender in mind, we will be able to start working with the Incredible Machine projects in a really fast manner.

How to know more about Blender 3D

If you want to follow the rest of the book, let's discuss a few resources to learn a bit more about Blender before we go any further. If you are an experienced Blender user, you may want to skip these tips because you probably already know them.

First thing to do is check out the Blender Wiki (`http://wiki.blender.org`), which is organized by the community of users. There you will find a lot of useful information about Blender, along with some links to great tutorials. However, if it's a book that you want, I can recommend my previous Blender book, *Blender 3D: Architecture, Buildings, and Scenery* about architectural visualization, with chapters detailing Blender basics. Another interesting reference would be the book, *Essential Blender*, published and organized by the Blender Foundation to introduce the software in general with no focus on any specific area.

Besides these resources, Blender has some great options to learn more about it with the open content projects, such as Big Buck Bunny and Yo Frankie! These are the open content projects from the Blender Foundation, which are a full-featured short animation and a professional-level game, respectively.

Both of them can be downloaded for free, and you can get the production files as well to learn more about the software and to see how the top-level artists work with Blender. To download the DVDs of the projects, visit the following links:

- `http://www.bigbuckbunny.org`
- `http://www.yofrankie.org`

If you really like these projects, I strongly recommend that you consider buying the DVDs to help finance the future projects of Blender.

I believe this is enough for an introduction. Let's get started with our first Incredible Machine project!

Summary

This chapter was a brief introduction to the main theme of the book, which is the creation of Incredible Machines with Blender 3D. We have learned the following:

- What Blender 3D is
- A bit about the Blender 3D history
- What an Incredible Machine is
- The workflow used in the book
- Previous knowledge that is required to follow the book
- How to learn more about Blender 3D

In the next chapter, we will begin working on the first project of the book and get ready to start using Blender to create Incredible Machines!

2
Modeling a Handgun

In this chapter, we will begin working on the first of three projects in this book—modeling of a handgun. Before we get started, let's point out a few important things about this project and find out why this particular object was chosen to be our first modeling project for the book. Here are a few points discussed in this chapter:

- How digital content creation is planned for games, animations, and advertisements
- Why we chose a hand weapon
- Project description
- Modeling techniques available for this project, and how to choose the best one
- Project workflow
- What the image will look like at the end

This will be a short chapter, but it will be an important one in order to get ready for what's coming next.

Briefing and concept

In all of our projects, we will try to follow the regular process for creating digital and art content that suits projects such as games or animations. If you are already experienced, or if you were part of a team involved with projects such as games, then you know that everything starts in a meeting with the art director of the project. At this meeting, the director shows some concepts about the project and talks about the objects, vehicles, or characters that he or she will need you to create.

At these meetings, the director already has the conceptual drawings of almost everything; all you have to do at the modeling stage is follow the concept and try to be as accurate as possible. We will not experience such kinds of events here in this book; however, we will follow the same workflow very closely. When we start a project, we always have to find some sort of reference image to follow; it will be easier and better to keep the shape and desired topology in mind along the modeling process.

With the reference images in hand, it will be a lot more clear to find the way in which all of the surfaces and materials behave with light at the surface of each object. Those reference images that we will be using in all of the projects work pretty much like the conceptual art used in project briefings. The conceptual art is an important stage in development of any project involving visual storytelling, and we have to learn how to deal with it if we want to work for this kind of industry.

Objectives

To focus on the production of this project, we can establish its objectives by using the same requirements of a job related to the games industry. This project, in particular, will be related to a sci-fi game, and our job will be the creation of parts of the machines for the advertisement campaign. With this objective in mind, we will be free of the boundaries related to the creation of 3D models for games, which are a bit annoying and difficult in many ways. For instance, if we had to create a model for the game, we would have to keep track of the polygon count and sometimes sacrifice the details of the model in order to keep a low level of polygons.

In a game project, all the rendering process would be handled by a *game engine*, generating all of the frames needed to represent the objects, scenarios, and characters in real time. As this type of rendering can demand a lot of resources from the computer hardware, we have to keep the poly count low in order to make the game compatible with a wide range of computers.

As our model will be used for advertisement, we will be able to create high poly models to be used in photo-real renderings. The project won't be related to animation—at least animation isn't mentioned in the objectives. We'll use the following objectives to guide us through the next chapters:

- Create parts of the machines and weapons used along the game
- Use the models for advertisement purposes
- Perform photo-real renderings
- Work on the model's details because there won't be a camera to show the objects' details

Why a hand weapon?

As you may have noticed, we are going to model a handgun because this object is an Incredible Machine! That was an easy one. But seriously, this first project gives you the opportunity to learn and practice intermediate to advanced modeling and composition techniques. The second and third projects, on the other hand, will require much more effort to be completed.

Before we talk more about the project, let's take a look at the first reference image of the project, which is as follows:

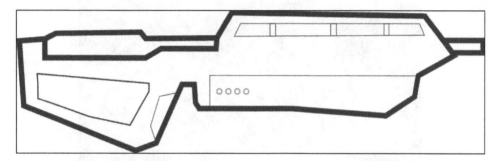

This model is relatively small in scale, but it has a lot of interesting details and shapes. The model may look a bit flat now; this is because it's still a reference image used only as a way to aid the modeling and visualization. Even if we have an already-created reference image, it doesn't mean that we can't add our own details and suggestions to the model, keeping in mind the overall concept. Remember that a project that had already some work on the concepts, most follow the guidelines of the concept, but other artists could use the concept to generate other materials and create another models. If we make big changes to the model, it will be reflected on all of the other parts of the project.

As we will be using a project-based learning approach, it's desirable that you make changes to the models in order to complete the learning process. Following the reference images at first sight is a good practice in which to engage. But, if you decide to follow the chapters again and create the machine one more time, try to make your own adjustments and improvements!

Parts of the model

In order to facilitate and organize the model, we will split the weapon into three different parts, which will be used as a reference for modeling; this could be used to create different versions of the same weapon as well, as it's only a matter of swapping the parts to get the shape and form of different objects. The following image shows us the different parts of the weapon:

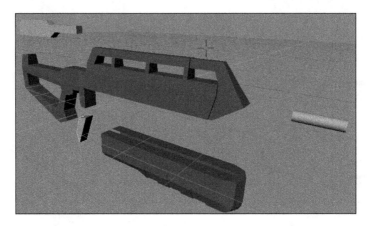

As we can see, we have the following parts:

- Energy Magazine and handgrip
- Stock and pistol grip
- Barrel, front sight, and inner barrel

Our Incredible Machine is made by all these parts, and if we want to create different sets of guns, all we have to do is create different versions of those parts for a new model. Splitting the object in parts will help us focus on small parts of the model and speed up the modeling.

Modeling workflow

This project, as well as almost all of the projects in this book will use the same workflow to make the process a bit easier. The workflow presented here splits the project into four steps, which are as follows:

1. Search for reference images
2. Modeling
3. Textures and materials
4. Light and effects

Some of the projects may have one extra task related with animation, but those parts of the workflow will be used for all of the projects.

Of those parts, the most important is the first one about the search for reference images. It's very hard for an artist to pick the shape of a model, and without any reference images or photos, create a 3D model out of nowhere.

The reference images used for the modeling of this project can be downloaded from Packt Publishing's website. After you have completed this project, I strongly recommend that you try modeling another handgun. This time, pick a handgun you saw in a sci-fi movie or a game, and make a few sketches of the basic shape.

If you manage to make the sketches directly on the computer, simply import this image into Blender and start working on the model. The sketches created by hand can be scanned and work just fine! Actually, I still prefer to hand-draw my sketches before I start working on a project because it's a lot quicker to make changes and experiment with different shapes.

With this first experience, I believe you will get the required knowledge to work on the advanced modeling projects.

Best modeling technique for this project

Of all the available modeling techniques from which to choose, this project will fit better with polygon modeling, also known as edge modeling. If we take a look at what the final model will look like, it's easy to understand the reason why this method is the best choice. But what are the main available modeling techniques? Several modeling techniques are available from poly modeling to metaballs, and all of them have positive and negative sides. Let's take a look at some of the main modeling techniques available today:

- **Poly modeling**: This is a type of modeling (also called edge modeling) works by the deformation and transformation of edges of a model to create new parts and shapes with a mesh object. For instance, we can start working on a simple plane and, by selecting an edge of the plane and with a sequence of extrudes, create a compound structure. With this technique, we can achieve a good level of detail in all of the models because the artist has control over the small areas of the model.

- **Subdivision modeling**: With the poly modeling technique, we start with a plane and transform the edges of the object. For the subdivision modeling technique, we use a primitive shape and apply the same tools and transformations to model something more complex. It's called subdivision because we add a lot of transformations into a cube, sphere, cone, or other primitive shape to build a more complex shape. For instance, we can start the modeling of a robot by creating a cube and extruding the faces of the cube until we get the rough shape for the robot. When the shape is created, we will add edges and new geometry to the model to subdivide it and create details.

- **Spline modeling**: All of the methods based in the transformation of geometry have a terrible limitation when the subject of the modeling has curved parts. For this reason, we have a modeling technique called spline modeling. With this technique, we will use Bezier curves to lead the modeling. These curves serve as a path for extrusion, or they can be used as a profile for tools that use revolving shapes to create surfaces.

- **NURBS modeling**: With the NURBS modeling technique, we can create curves that are used to build surfaces. The curves are created and positioned to represent the basic shape of the object, and when everything is placed correctly, we connect the curves to create surfaces between them.

With these descriptions in mind, it's easy to understand that we choose Poly modeling to be able to control small details of the modeling process. If you don't remember or have never used this technique, it's easy to understand. All we have to do is select a few edges of the 3D models and extrude them. That's all! It would be great if the process of modeling with polygons was easy to execute, just as it is easy to explain. The difficult part is to organize the topology of the model until we get the shape of the object that we are trying to model. And at this point, the artist's skills can make a difference.

For a few of the model's details, we will be using curves and modifiers as well to get to the final result.

Effects and rendering

It would be fairly simple to model only the handgun, but as a part of the concept that makes this an Incredible Machine, let's put this thing to work! As you may be wondering, a handgun is best used to fire up some laser blasts or other projectiles. Well, you get the point!

The last chapter will be about effects and composition to make it look as if the weapon is really working. So, we will be using a few tricks with particles and halos to give life to our Incredible Machine.

Now that we know more about our first project, let's jump into Blender and work on our Incredible Machine.

Summary

In this chapter, we learned a bit more about our first project and how important it is to achieve our objectives with the book. Here is a quick summary of the topics discussed in the chapter:

* The reason we chose a handgun for our first project
* What the final image of the project will look like
* How many chapters it will take to finish the project
* Modeling workflow
* Which modeling technique will be used to work on the project
* Effects and composition tricks we can use to generate the final image

In the next chapter, we will work on the modeling of the weapon using poly modeling techniques.

3
Polygon Modeling of the Weapon

Now that we have passed through all the initial phases of the project, working with the concept and idea of the first project, we can finally begin working on it. This chapter will guide you through the first steps of the modeling by using concept drawings to create a base model in Blender. The base model will be very important to add details and upgrade the first flat surfaces into something more complex.

With the base model created, we will be able to analyze the shape of our model and evaluate the next steps of the project. We can even decide to make changes to the project because new ideas may appear when we see the object in 3D rather than in 2D.

In this phase, some professionals and studios may use sculptors or designers to work on real clay models, sculpted to give the creation team a good idea of the object. It would be great to have this kind of resource, but I believe that the use of clay to get to this level of evaluation is out of scope of this book. So, we will stick to Blender as our only design tool.

Starting with a background image

The first step to start the modeling is to add the reference image as the background of the Blender 3D view. To do that, we can go to the **View** menu in the 3D view and choose **Background Image**. The background image in Blender appears only when we are at an orthogonal or Camera view.

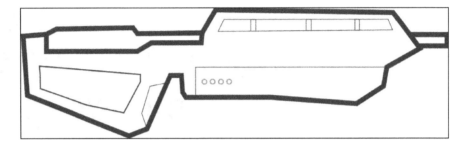

The background image is a simple black and white drawing of the weapon, but it will be a great reference for modeling.

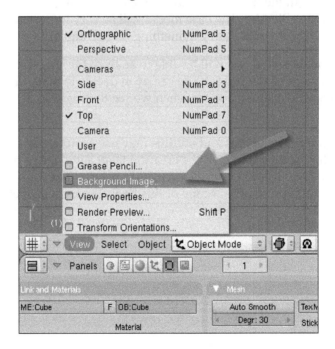

Before we go any further, it's important to point out a few things about the **Background Image** menu. We can make some adjustments to the image if it doesn't fit our Blender view:

- **Use**: With this button turned on, we will use the image as a background. If you want to hide the image, just turn it off and the image will disappear.
- **Blend**: The blend slider will control the transparency of the image. If you feel that the image is actually blocking your view of the whole model, making it a bit transparent may help.
- **Size**: As the name says, we can control the scale of the image.
- **X and Y offset**: With this option, we will be able to move the image in the X or Y axis to place it in a specific location.

After clicking on the **Use** button, just hit the load button and choose the image to be used as a reference. If you don't have the image used in this example, visit Packt Publishing's website and download the project files for this book.

If you've never used a reference image in Blender, it is important to note that the reference images appear only in 3D view when we are using the orthographic view or the camera view mode. It works only in the top, right, left, front, and other orthographic views. If you hit 5 and change the view to perspective, the image will disappear. By using the middle mouse button or the scroll to rotate the view, the image disappears. However, it's still there and we can see the image again by changing the view to an orthogonal or camera view.

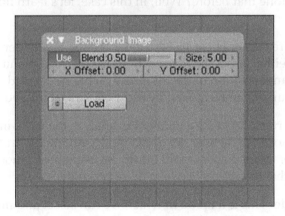

Make the image more transparent by using the Blend control. It will help in focusing on the model instead of the image. A value of 0.25 will be enough to help in the modeling without causing confusion.

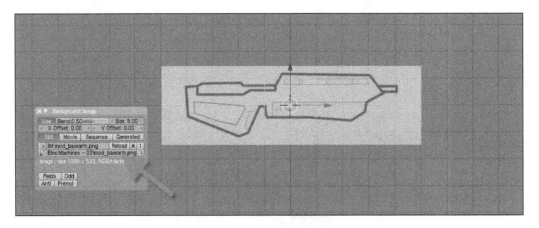

Using subdivision to model

With the reference image placed in 3D view, we can start modeling. This next part of the chapter will seem a bit repetitive, but it will use a common technique for polygon modeling, which is the adjustment of the model to the lines of the reference image. If you have already worked with this kind of modeling, it won't be hard to follow. What if I've never done that before? Well, in this case, let's learn how to handle a modeling like this one.

The first step is to create a cube, or use the default cube of Blender. To create objects in Blender, we can either press the Space bar or use the Add menu. All of the objects are created at the same position of the 3D cursor, which is the little target we see in the 3D view. This cursor can be moved by right-clicking at any point in the 3D view.

Before we go any further, let's take a moment to analyze the work modes in Blender. Some of the work modes in Blender are object mode, edit mode, and sculpt mode. For the modeling part of this project, we will mostly be using object mode and edit mode. Let's take a look at the differences between these two modes:

- **Object mode**: This is a mode in which we can select and manipulate the objects completely. The object mode is the best work mode in which to make object transformations, such as move, scale, and rotate. In object mode, we can't select the sub-parts of the 3D model like vertices, edges, and faces. As this type doesn't allow us to change the vertices, edges, and faces of an object, it's the safest way to make transformations without accidentally deforming the object.

- **Edit mode**: In edit mode, we will be able to select and change the vertices, edges, and faces of an object, which is why we will always use this type of work mode to apply changes to objects.

There are two ways to change the work mode between object and edit in Blender 3D, which involves the use of the *Tab* key or the work mode selector, placed in the header of the 3D view. This selector is placed below the 3D view right next to the text menu options in the header.

To use work modes in Blender properly, follow these two simple rules:

1. All of the objects should be created only in object mode. If an object is created in edit mode, it will be added to the object that is already being edited. It would be something like adding the geometry to the object, and at the end, we will have a compound shape formed by a lot of different objects.

2. Right after the creation of an object, check to see if the work mode didn't change to edit mode. In the past versions of Blender, the swapping to edit mode always took place when an object was created. In the latest version, however, it remains in object mode by default; still, it's always a good idea to check it to avoid problems with the modeling.

Select this cube, and with the scale, change the size of the cube until it fits the area pointed in the following image:

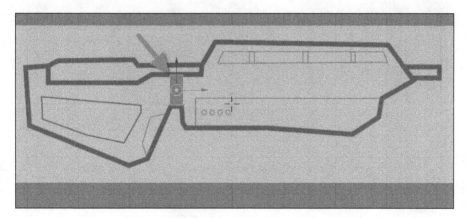

Another way to start the project is with a simple mesh plane. A few artists prefer to use a plane to model because it's easier to control and has fewer vertices to manipulate. With a plane, we would have to create half of the object and create a mirrored copy with the mirror modifier at the end of the modeling.

If you don't remember how to do that, just use the *S* key to scale the object. Additionally, to make a scale in a specific axis, use the *X* and *Y* keys to constrain the scale to the X and Y axis.

Now it's time for our first extrusion! Select the vertices pointed in the image below using the *B* key to make a border selection. Make sure you are in with wireframe as your dram mode. If you are not in wireframe mode when the selection is made, your vertices at the back of the model won't be selected.

There is an option called **Occlude background geometry** that is turned on by default. If you want to work on shade view, make sure this option is always turned on. Otherwise, you will have some troubles with the selection of objects occluded by faces near the camera.

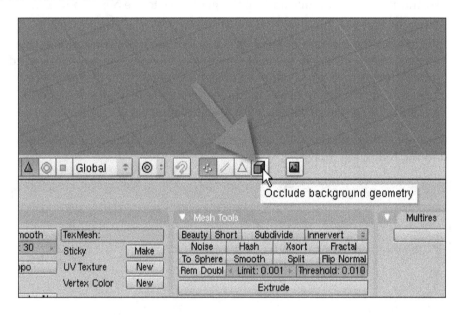

Some useful keyboard shortcuts for this type of modeling:

To change the work mode use the *Tab* key. The selection mode can be switched with the *Ctrl+Tab* keys, and the transformation widget can be turned on and off with the *Ctrl+Space* keys.

With the view mode switched to wireframe, select the vertices pointed in the following image and extrude them with the *E* key:

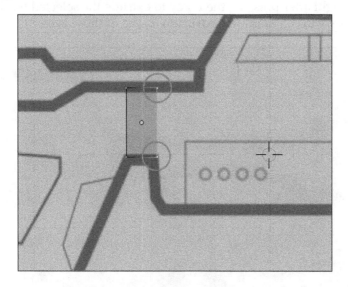

If anything goes wrong with the extrusion, we can press the *Esc* key to cancel the operation. If the extrude has already created some geometry, the *Esc* key will cancel the operation but it won't erase the new faces. In this case, it's always good to use the *Ctrl+Z* keys to undo the extrusion.

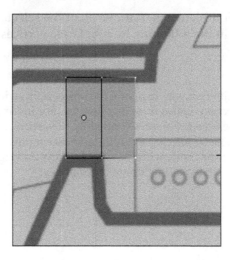

The extrusion will be used again to create more geometry for the base model. This time, select the vertices at the bottom, and make two extrusions to the lower part of the object. Right after pressing the *E* key to extrude the selected vertices, press the *X*, *Y* or *Z* keys to constrain the extrusion to one of those axes.

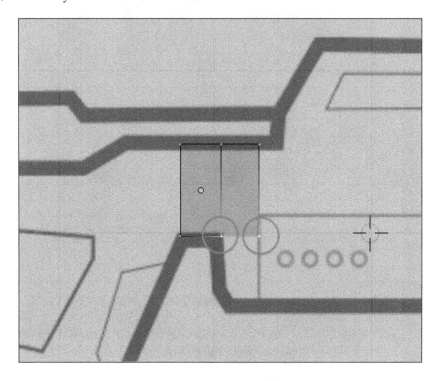

After the last extrusion is created, remove all of the selected vertices and select only the vertices pointed in the following image. These vertices will be moved just a bit to the right.

A different way to model the object is by switching between the selection modes from time to time. For instance, when we have to select a set of faces formed by 12 vertices, sometimes it's better and faster to select everything in face mode. Just change the selection mode with the *Ctrl+Tab* keys and right-click on each face while holding down the *Shift* key.

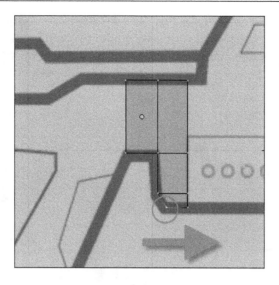

Working with polygons requires a great deal of knowledge to place and manipulate the edges of a model. Sometimes, we will have to add or remove new edges to be able to work with it. For instance, we have to add an extra loop to our model; otherwise, we won't be able to create another extrusion in the right place.

In Blender, these new loops can be added with the **Face Loop Cut** tool. Make sure that you are still in edit mode and press the *Ctrl+R* keys. It will add a magenta line to the model, where you should choose the position and orientation of the new edge loops. Place the new loops in a way that it stays aligned with the guideline of the reference image, pointed in the following image:

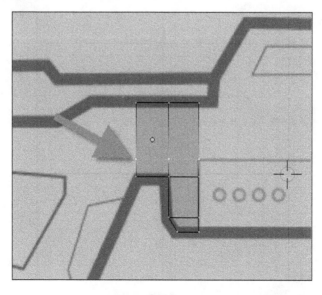

With the new edge loop created, we can carry on with the modeling. Select the top vertices on the right of the model, as shown in the following image. We will create a set of sequential extrusions that will end up in a model like the one in the next three images. In the third image, we will have to select the upper vertices and move them to the right.

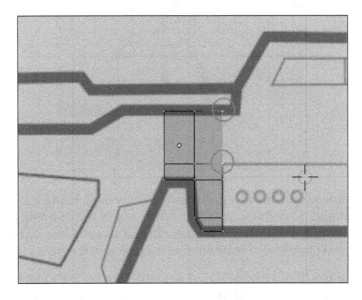

Make sure that you use the *B* key and draw a selection window to add all of the vertices to the extrusion.

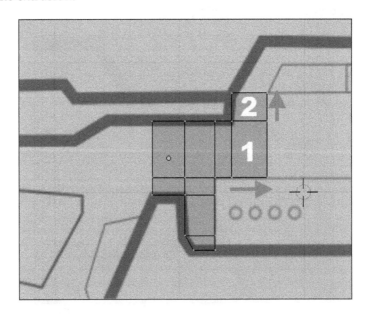

Or, change the select mode to face to right-click on each face of the mode. This action, however, would require a small rotation on the view.

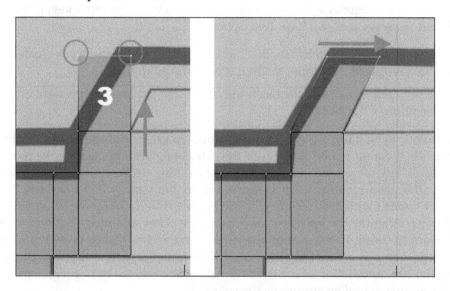

Here, we encounter the same problem. We need an extra cut to keep the extrusions. So, use the *Ctrl+R* keys to add an extra loop, as shown in the following image:

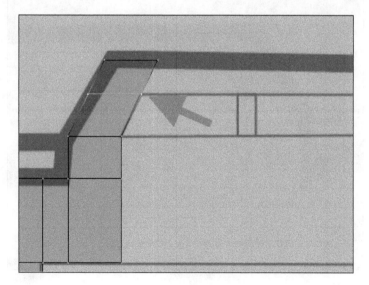

The next step would be to select the vertices of the model and carry out another extrusion. But, in this case, we have to work on a small problem. The faces of the model are not orthogonal with the guidelines. When we press the *E* key, it won't be aligned. To solve that, we have two options:

1. Create all of the extrusions first, and after all of the geometry is created, move the vertices of the model to align it with the guidelines.

2. Use a trick to extrude the faces and cancel the transformation right after the creation of the faces.

For this case, we will use a trick. It's quite simple to use; simply select the vertices and extrude them normally. Right after the extrusion, without clicking the mouse, press the *Esc* key to quit the transformation of the new vertices. When we press the *Esc* key, all transformations, such as move, rotate, and scale will be canceled, but the geometry created with the extrude will still be there overlapping the selected objects. Immediately after the *Esc* key is pressed, press the *G* key and move the new vertices. If you want to constrain the motion the vertices in the X or Y axis, press the X or Y keys once when you are moving the vertices. It's quite important that you press the *G* key after the cancellation of the transformation because the new geometry created with the extrusion will be automatically selected.

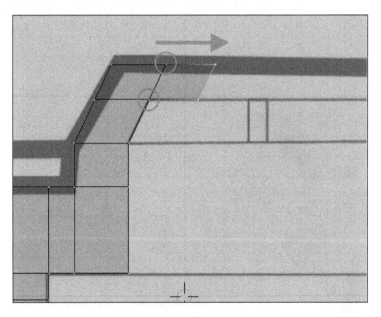

Let's continue modeling with the selection of the vertices circled in the following image:

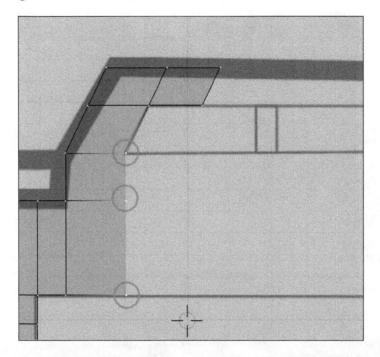

The extrusion of these vertices will create a new part of our model but, again, we face a small problem. The problem is that the new faces are completely out of alignment. If we follow the extrusions the way they are, the alignment will need to be made by hand, which is not very good. By the end of the modeling, we will certainly have some troubles with the edge loops.

So, here is the trick! Select all of the faces that you want to align in the same plane. When all of the vertices are selected, press the *S* key to scale all of the faces. While you are still scaling down the vertices, press the key corresponding to the perpendicular axis for the planes of the vertices. In this example, I will press the *Y* key once.

After pressing the *Y* key, press the *0* key once on your keyboard. This will set the scale size to zero and will flatten out the distance between all of the vertices.

Here is the result of the use of the trick in our example:

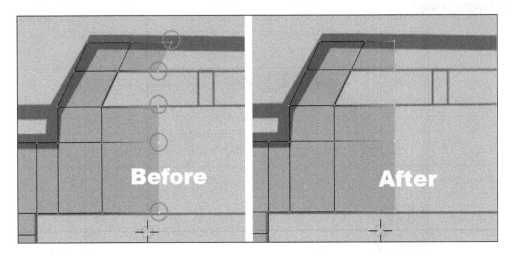

It will be quite easy to move the aligned vertices a bit to the right and then extrude the planes a few times—to be more exact, seven times. Use the lines of the reference image as a guide.

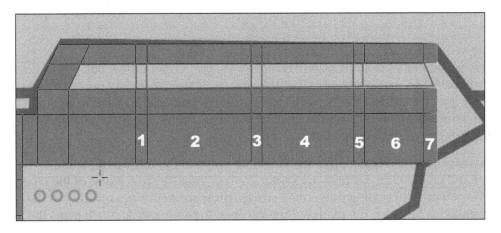

The right side of the model has a lot of non-orthogonal lines and planes, and to model those parts, we will use a simple move transformation. Select the vertices pointed in the following image, and move them to the right. To finish these last adjustments, select the vertices pointed in the image on the right, and move them until they get aligned with the lines of the reference image. For this type of action, everything must be done by eye, without the aid of a specialized tool.

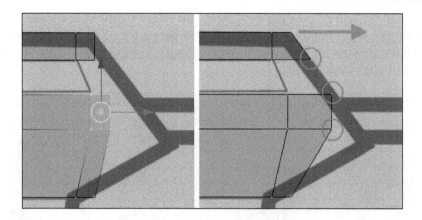

The next step is to work on the connections on the top of the model. We can rotate the view of the model for a better view by using the scroll or middle mouse button. By doing that, the background image will disappear, but it's only because we left an orthogonal view.

To make those connections, we will use a tool in Blender called **Skin Faces/Edge-Loops**. This tool connects two selected faces and makes the required faces and edges connect automatically.

If you want to make this part of the editing process easier, change the select mode to faces and select, with a single right-click of the mouse, the faces pointed in the following image. When the faces are selected, press the *F* key and choose **Skin Faces/Edge-Loops**.

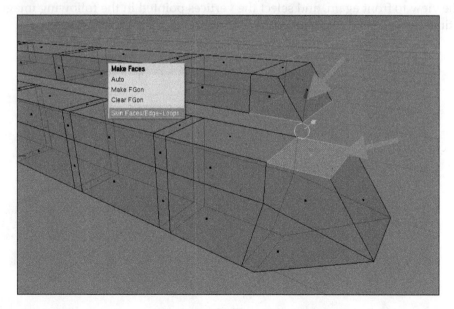

By doing that, we will be creating new faces and edges required to connect the faces. It's quite simple and a handy way to create new geometry. With the same tool, select and repeat the process for the other three required connections until our model looks like the following image:

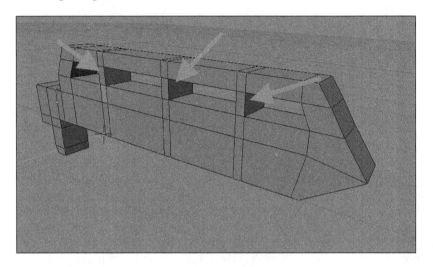

With this last editing, we can leave the top front of the model and turn our attention to the back. Now it's time to work on the hand wrap of the gun.

Modeling the hand wrap

Set the view to front again, and select the vertices pointed in the following image. This time we will need two extrusions.

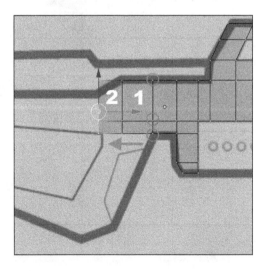

Select the vertices in the top-left corner of the model, and move them down to align them to the image. Then, select the other three vertices shown in the following image and extrude them once:

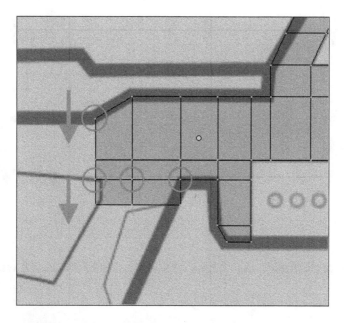

As the extruded geometry doesn't fit the guides of our reference image, we will have to select and move the lower vertices and place them as shown in the following image. They don't have to be exactly in the same position, but they should be placed in such a way that the shape of the model looks like our reference image.

 Remember that you can also select the vertices with the brush select tool. Press the *B* key twice, and then you will be able to paint the selection.

Right after you place the vertices in their new positions, make another extrusion. By the end of the extrusion, try to place the lower vertices aligned with the right side of the guidelines.

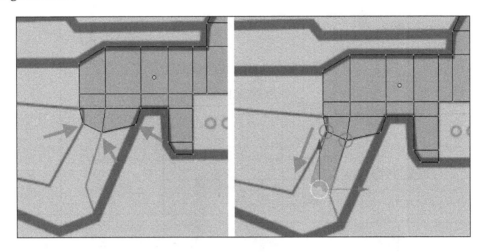

Just by looking at the image, you'll notice that one side of the model won't be aligned. So, select the vertices on the left or right (any one that isn't aligned with the image) and move it until it gets aligned.

By now, the work will be a repetition of extrusions until we have our model created. Select the vertices pointed in the next images, and extrude them until you get the final shape. At this point in the project, you should be familiar with the technique.

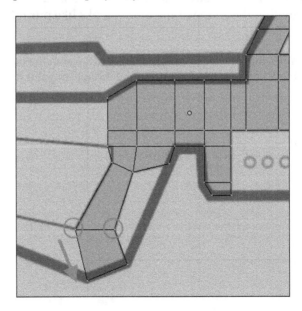

It's important to remember that for those operations, most of the alignment of the objects with the reference image is done by eye.

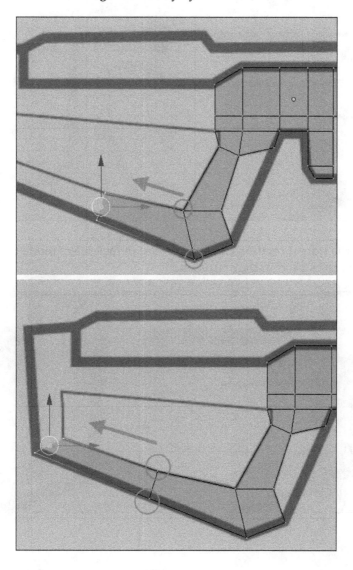

At the end of each extrusion, use the *S* key to set the size of the new geometry until it fits with the reference image.

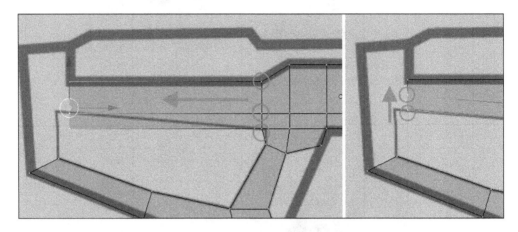

If you prefer, the transformation can be executed in face select mode to speed up the selection of the faces used in the extrusion.

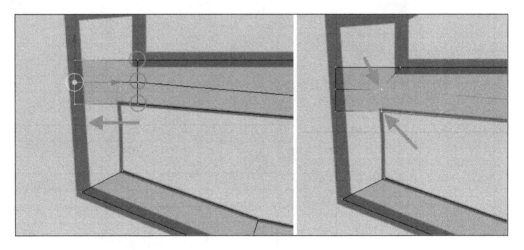

Here, we'll use the **Skin Faces/Edge-Loops** option again to connect the two selected faces. Sometimes, the faces created with this option will be generated with a **Set Smooth** option selected. This may cause the faces to look odd and have a different set of shading from the other faces. To make it look exactly the same as other faces of the model, select the created faces and click on the **Set Solid** button.

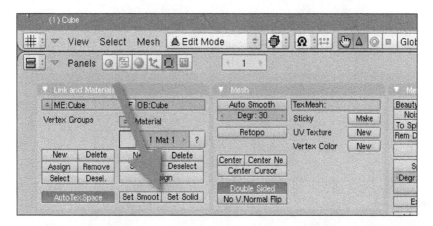

If you don't know where this button is located, you will find it in the **Editing** panel.

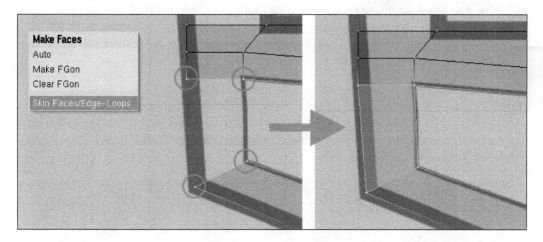

After the **Skin Faces/Edge-Loops** option is applied, the shade of the object will look a bit strange. This is because the smooth option of Blender is being used. Use the **Set Solid** option to make the faces appear in flat shade mode.

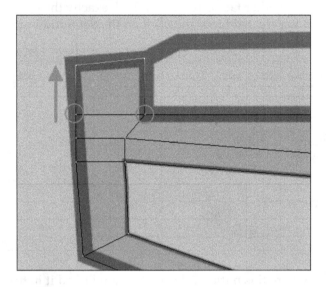

A big part of the modeling is complete, but there are a few parts of the weapon missing. Our next task is to create additional parts of the gun, such as a detail for the hand wrap and the energy tank. For this project, we will create different objects for those parts to make our modeling easier.

As you can see in the following image, we have created a big part of the gun with a well-organized topology and a fairly clean mesh, which is represented by a minimum number of faces and vertices, made only by quad faces. This type of mesh can be easily edited later by using subdivisions and new extrudes, which is a good reason to keep it as clean as possible.

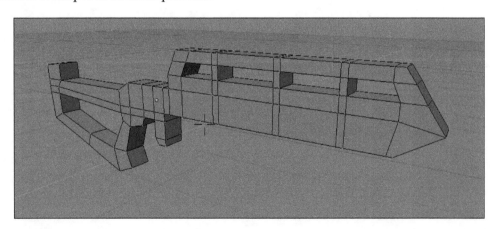

Modeling the small and removable parts

The first part that we will model is the energy tank for the gun, which will be placed in the lower front section of the weapon. The energy tank has two functions: It works as an energy source and serves as a place to hold the gun with both hands.

In order to place and align two different objects, a few extra tools that we haven't used before will be required. The 3D cursor, for example, is the most powerful way in which Blender places objects exactly where we want.

To begin, select the model that we've already created and try to select the vertices pointed in the following image. When the vertices are selected, press the *Shift+S* keys to call the snap menu, and choose **Cursor -> Selection** to make the 3D cursor jump to the position of the vertices.

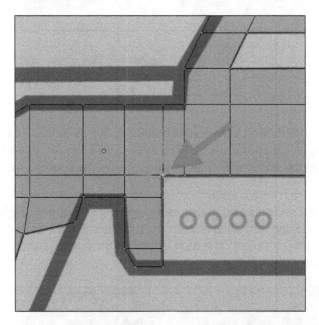

With the 3D cursor placed at the right position, change the work mode to object. Add a new cube object and move the cube until it gets placed in the positions shown in the image below. Note that the cube is moved in object mode. For this move, we can use either grid snapping or vertex snapping. If you want to use the grid snapping, hold down the *Ctrl* key while you move the cube using the grid lines to place the cube at the correct position.

Another way to snap the cube in the right position is by using a tool called vertex snap. With this snap option, we can place objects using other objects as a reference with a simple drag-and-drop action. You will find the vertex snap tool in the 3D view header represented by a small magnet icon. By clicking on this icon, you will enable the vertex snap mode and disable the grid snap.

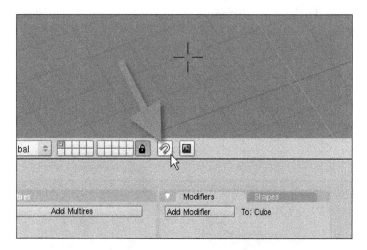

This tool uses the interaction between two objects. For instance, we can select a sphere model to place it above a table. The sphere will be moved and placed in a position related to the table, which makes the sphere the source object and the table the target object.

When the magnet icon is clicked, a few extra options will appear right next to the button. The first one will determine if the objects should be aligned with a rotation to the snapping target. The next option allows us to choose from several snapping elements.

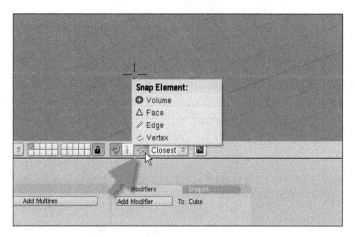

There are basically four different snapping elements, which are as follows:

1. Volume
2. Face
3. Edges
4. Vertex

Each one of the options will use an element of the target object to snap the object. The last three will use faces, edges, and vertices. But, with the first option, we will use the whole volume of the model to snap. If you want to use this snap option, a good choice for this will be the vertex.

At the last part of the vertex snapping, we will find the following four options for the snap mode:

1. **Active**: With this option, we will use the active object as the reference for snapping.
2. **Median**: The median point of the source object will be used for snapping.
3. **Center**: Here we will use the center point of the object for snapping.
4. **Closest**: This last option will use the closest part of the object used as a source of snapping.

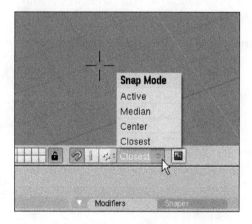

For instance, if we choose vertex as the snapping element and center as the snap mode, when the source object is selected, the center of this object will snap to the vertex of the target object that is closest to the mouse cursor.

To use the vertex snap, select the source object and press the *Ctrl* key to move the object. A small white circle will appear at the target object pointing out the position of the snapping.

Using any of the options presented, we will have (at the end) the cube placed at the position shown in the following image:

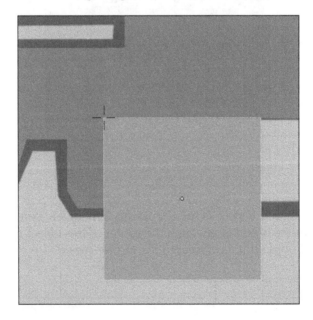

The process now will be similar to what we have been doing all along. Select the vertices of the cube and with the extrusion and transformation tools, subdivide the cube until it fits the shape of the reference image. You may have to make adjustments to the shape of the cube in the process, but it won't require any new technique.

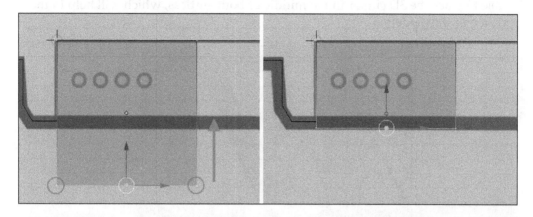

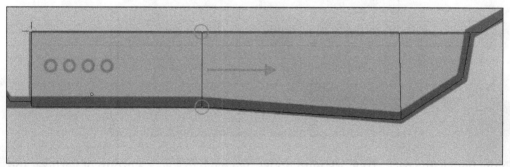

Using hooks to place and align objects

The 3D cursor doesn't work all alone, and together with some other tools, such as hooks, we can work out almost any kind of alignment needed in Blender. Hooks in Blender are mostly used to create vertex animations, and for that they work really great. But here, we will use them to move parts of our model and make them fit in the right places.

Before we create our first hook, we need something to work on, and that's why the first task is to create a new cube. Place the 3D cursor at the same position shown in the following image, next to the hand wrap of the gun. Use the *B* key to select the vertex, and both vertices of the model will be selected. With the snap option, we will be able to place the 3D cursor in the middle of both vertices, which will help in the next step of the modeling.

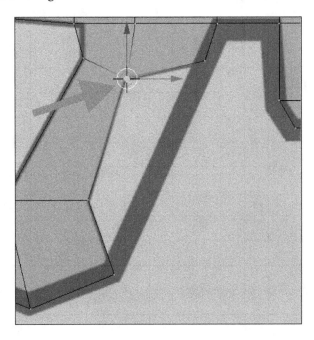

Now here is the trick. To work with hooks, we have to select a group of vertices and assign to them a hook. When we move the hook, all of the vertices connected with this hook will move with it. It may seem silly, but we can actually place vertices in hard places using this tool.

Let's apply our knowledge of hooks in this project. After the placing of the 3D cursor, create a new cube. While you are still in edit mode, select the vertices in the lower left corner of the cube. Press the *Ctrl+H* keys to add a hook to those vertices, choose the **Add, New Empty** option to create a helper object called empty, and assign the hook to this new empty.

An empty object is a type of helper that can be used in a lot of situations, from animations to modeling. It can't be rendered, nor can it receive materials, which makes it perfect to use as a reference for modeling and deforming models with hooks.

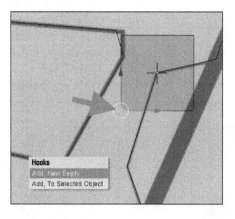

Repeat the same process for all the vertices in the other three corners of the cube. Make sure that each corner has its own hook.

With the hooks created, we will be able to move the vertices of the model to their right positions. Select the bigger model that was created in the first part of this chapter, and select the vertices where the 3D cursor is placed in the following image. When the 3D cursor is placed, select the empty related to the upper-right corner of the cube, press *Shift+S*, and choose **Selection -> Cursor**. You will see the whole set of vertices jump right into position.

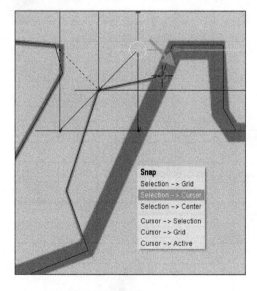

We can repeat the same process for the empties in the other three corners of the model. By the end, the four corners of the cube will be placed in the right position with a minimum amount of work; it will require only a few keyboard short cuts.

The empty objects will still be there, holding down the position of our cube. Every time we work with hooks, a set of modifiers will be created to control the amount of influence and will allow us to remove the hooks from all, or a single vertex. If you want, you can erase the empty and maintain the position of the vertices, select the modifiers, and click on the **Apply** button. After that, the deformation created by the hooks will be applied to the vertices, and then all empties can be erased without losing the effect.

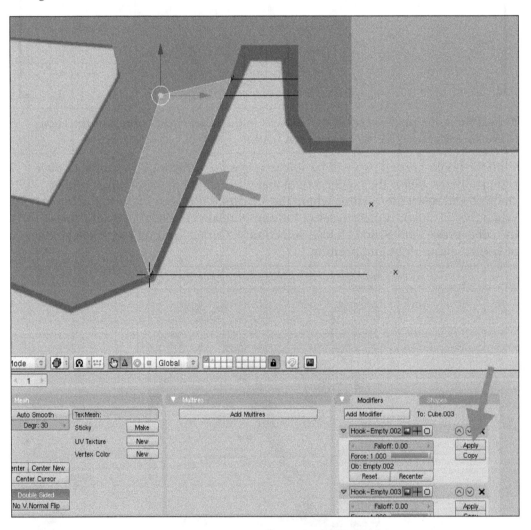

To improve the hand wrap, just make the last created cube a bit smaller in the Y axis.

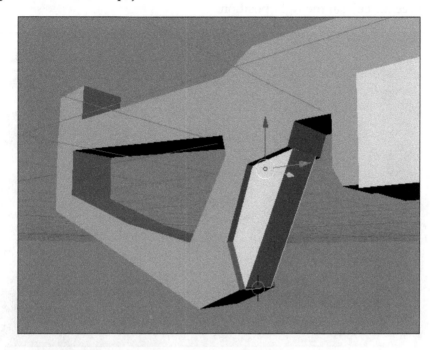

Finally, we can work on the last part of the modeling for this first phase. By now, you will know how to handle this type of modeling. Just add another cube, and by using the tools that we've just learned, such as hooks and the 3D cursor, we can create an object that fits the upper-left corner of the image.

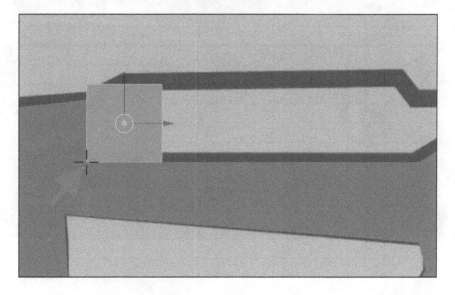

Just as a reminder, we can use either the snap available to the 3D cursor or the vertex snap to place the cube at the right position.

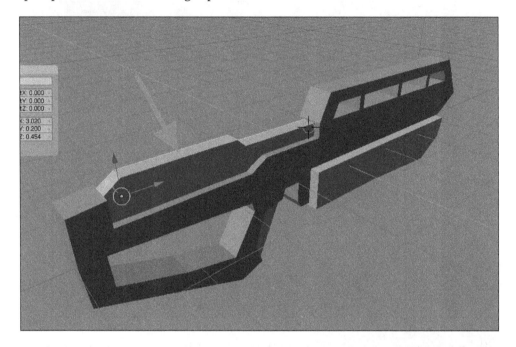

The final touch will be the addition of a cylinder located at the front of our gun.

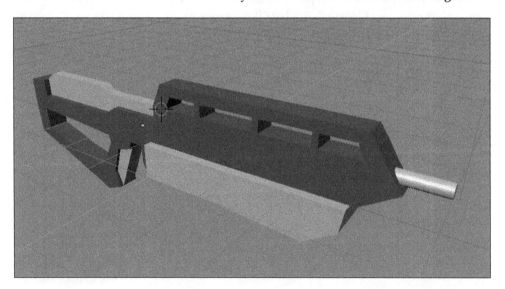

Our project is in its early stages, but we've learned the tools necessary to complete the base model in a few simple steps. In the next chapters, the challenge will be to add details and materials to the object. This is only the beginning!

Summary

In this last chapter, we began creating the basis for our first project. All of the modeling was based on subdivision, and for that we used the most common tools in Blender to achieve our goals.

So far, we have learned how to do the following:

- Add a reference image as a background in Blender
- Set up and configure a background image
- Model and transform a mesh by using the background image as a guide
- Select and flatten vertices in a unique plane
- Use the edge loop tool to connect two separate faces
- Use the face loop cut tool to add new edges to meshes
- Use the 3D cursor tool to align and snap faces and vertices
- Use the hook tool and the 3D cursor to add more precision to transformations
- Use vertex snapping

4

Adding Details

In the previous chapters, we started working on our first Incredible Machine model, which is a handgun. Now, with the base model ready, it's time to add a few more details before we go further with textures and materials. The base model that we had created will work much like a proxy model used for animations, or something like a low poly version of the model.

Tools and techniques for detailing

To create this model, we are using a very common technique called **poly modeling**. The process of adding details to a model with poly modeling is all about managing the edges and loops of a model. For instance, if we have a flat surface and we want to add a crease to this surface, the best solution would be to select a small plane and extrude it down. But, what if this plane doesn't exist? Enter the modeler's best friend—the cut loop tool!

As we will see along this chapter and the other projects, the tools required to create detailed models are the ones that we use every day; it's just a matter of finding the right sequence and determining the best place to add creases or other small modeling details.

Face normals

Before we begin, we should note an important feature for this project and all other modeling projects involving poly modeling: the **face normals**. Every face we create has something called normals pointing in a perpendicular direction from the face. The face normals set the visible side of the faces and can be decisive to export the model later to external renderers like YafaRay. Even if this is not a primary concern now, the normals of an object can always be verified with a simple button available in the editing panel of Blender. The following screenshot shows the location of the button:

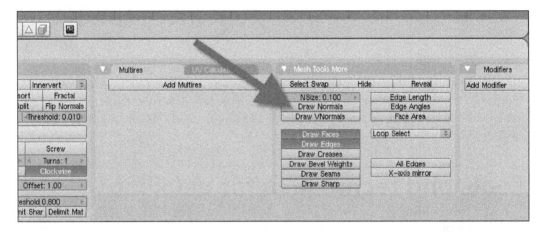

Press the **Draw Normals** button and the normals will appear as small lines pointing out from the center of the faces in the 3D view of Blender.

If a model turns out to have the normals pointing toward the wrong direction, we can always change the normals with an option available in the specials menu. In edit mode, press the *W* key and the specials menu will appear. There we will find an option called **Flip Normals**, which will actually flip the normals of all the selected faces the moment this option is activated. The same option is also available in the **Mesh Tools** menu in the editing panel.

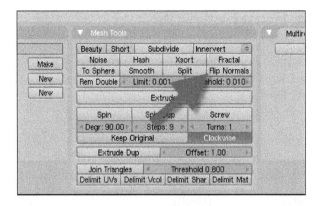

Besides the **Flip Normals** option, we have two keyboard short cuts that can help to manage the normals of a 3D model. By pressing *Ctrl+N* keys, we can force the recalculation of the normals pointing to the outside of the model, and by using the *Ctrl+Shift+N* keys, we can force the normals to point to the inside of the model. Both of the tools can be found in the **Normals** menu located at the **Mesh** menu, which appears when we are editing a mesh object in the edit mode.

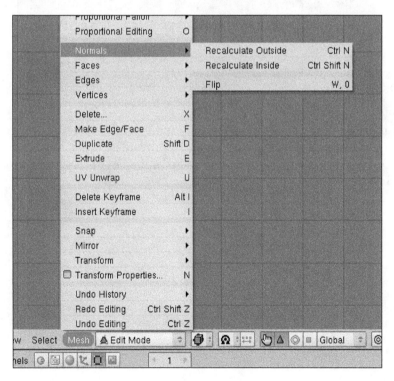

Adding the handgrip

In the previous chapter, we split the model into several different parts, which is a great way to work without interfering with the modeling. Our first task with the base model will be in the lower part of the gun, where a shooter would hold the weapon. This part of the model is too flat, so we will start by adding a few more surfaces and places to get a grip when the shooter holds the weapon.

The first step is to select only the lower part of the model and hide the rest of the gun, moving it to another layer. Just select the model and press the *M* key in object mode. Choose a layer that is turned off, and the selected model will be hidden.

Leave the part, displayed in the following image, off the selection.

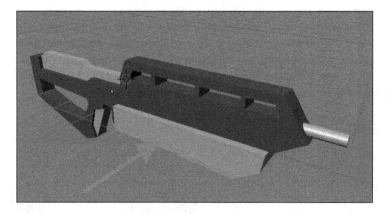

With only this part of the base model visible, change your view to front with the *1* key (numpad), and create a mesh circle with eight sides. If the circle is not aligned with your 3D view, rotate it until the alignment of the object looks just like the following image:

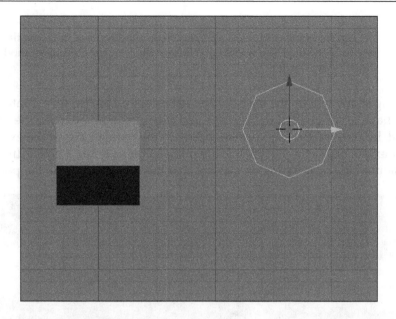

This circle will be used to create the bottom of the model and make it rounded.

Right after adding the circle, scale it until the size of the object is near the same proportion as the one created in the last chapter. When the size of the model is set, change the work mode to edit and select only the three top vertices of the circle, and erase them by using the X key. By now, the resulting model should be an arc. Select the two top vertices of the arc and extrude the vertices until we get a model that looks like this:

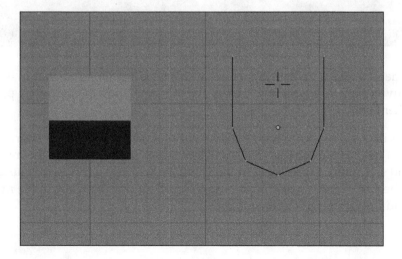

We can set Blender to select vertices, edges, and faces at the same time. Just hold the *Shift* key while you click on the icon for each select mode on the 3D view header.

The resulting shape will be the basis for the entire object, and to turn it into a 3D shape, we have to select all of the vertices and extrude them. To make the extrusion orthogonal, hold down the key corresponding to the parallel axis of the extrusion. If the proper axis is not clear, use the middle mouse button to see a better direction of the extrusion. In the next figure, we can see that the direction was in the positive X.

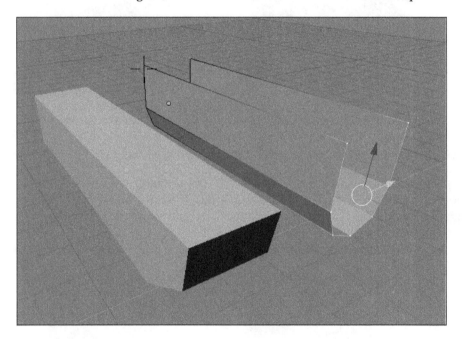

Since the new model is proportionate, we won't need the block created in the last chapter anymore. If you want to clean up the 3D view, hide the model by placing it in another layer.

Now, we will begin working with the loop cut tool. Using the *Ctrl+R* short cut, add a first cut at the back of the gun; it doesn't have to be in the center of the model, but instead a bit more to the back. In the front, we will add a few more cuts. After pressing the *Ctrl+R* keys, use your mouse to scroll, or use the + key in the numpad. This will add multiple cuts to the model.

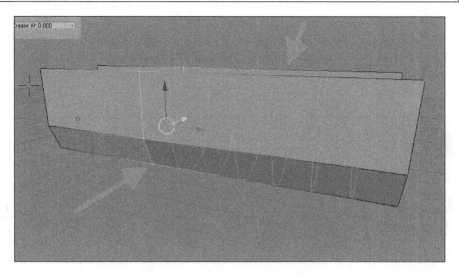

 If we confirm the loop cut tool with the middle mouse button, the new cut will always be created in the center of the selected face. Use the middle button when the magenta line appears, choose the direction of the cut, and confirm with the middle button.

The result of the cuts will look something like this:

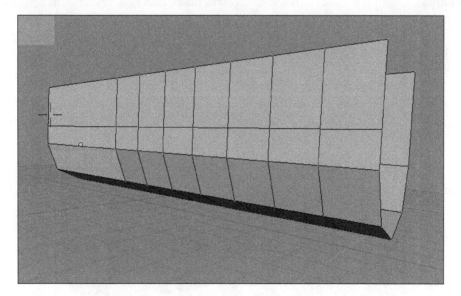

Now is a good time to erase half the model and make a copy of it with the mirror modifier. Select one of the sides of the model and add a mirror modifier, which is an incredible tool to work with symmetrical models. Remember to press the **Do Clipping** button to make the modifier cut all of the geometry that overlaps the shape of the model:

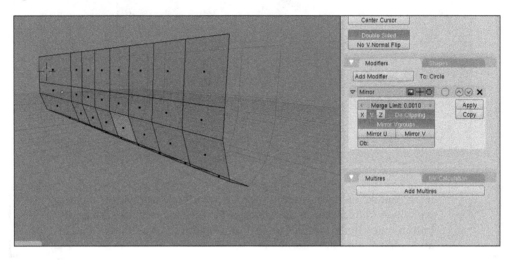

Let's begin working on the details of the model by selecting only a few faces from the lower areas. Change the work mode to faces to make this task easier, and select the faces pointed in the following image:

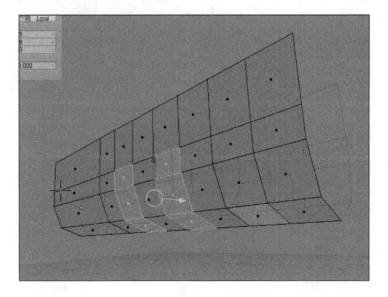

With the faces selected, just press the *X* key and erase them.

We had to select two groups of faces and erase them in the previous task. Now we have to select another group of three faces, but on the right side of the model. You don't have to follow the same pattern; just select another group of faces and extrude them inside the shape of the model. This is another important part of detailing models, especially if these models have a lot of creases. Right after the first extrusion, scale down the faces, and repeat the process one more time.

The resulting model should look like this:

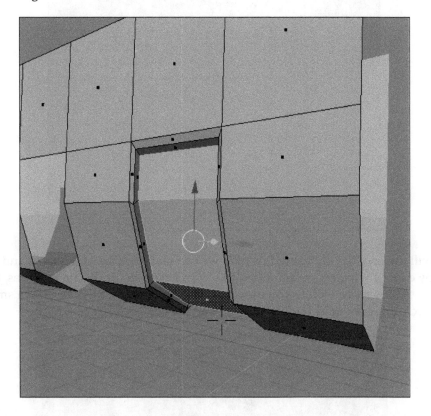

What about the holes? With this part of the model ready, we will be able to copy it to fill in the holes. A new snapping tool has been recently added in Blender; it's a great help for this kind of modeling task.

To use this new snapping tool, we have to press the icon of a small magnet on the 3D view header. Right after selecting the faces pointed in the next figure, press the magnet icon.

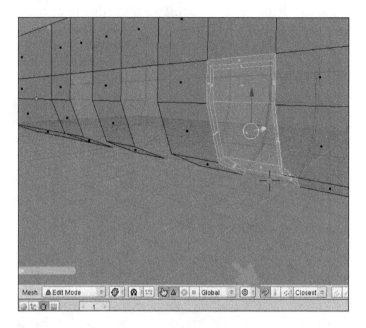

What will this tool do? By using this tool, we can make a copy of the faces and place the copy exactly where we want. Press the *Shift+D* keys to duplicate the faces, and hold down the *Ctrl* key while you move the faces near the hole. Wait until a small white circle appears, marking the spot to drop the copied faces.

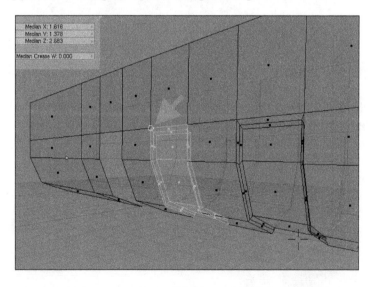

Repeat the same process to copy the faces one more time, and we won't have anymore holes left.

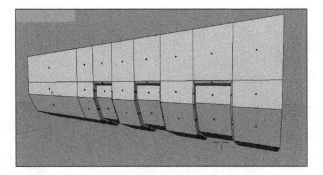

Using the spin tool to close a model

Let's move on to the front of the model and close that big opening by adding some faces there. But, since the model is rounded in the lower part, we will have to use the spin tool to create a rounded set of faces and close the model.

The spin tool uses the position of the 3D cursor to create new edges, so it's quite important to place the cursor before anything else. Select the vertex point in the following figure. While pressing the *Shift+S* short cut keys, place the 3D cursor in the same position as the vertex with the **Cursor | Selection** option.

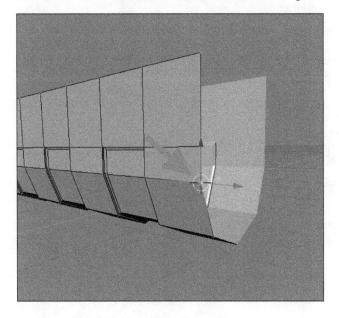

Now, select the three edges that are shown in the next figure. Keep in mind that we have to make the view perpendicular to the spin to make it work. For instance, in this example, the view must be set to **Front** before the use of spin.

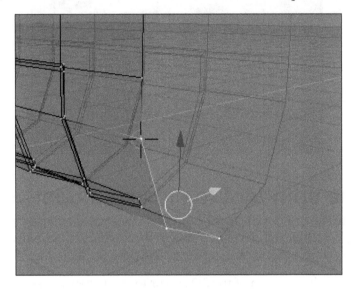

Here are the settings for this spin tool:

- 90 Degrees
- 5 Steps
- Clockwise button: OFF

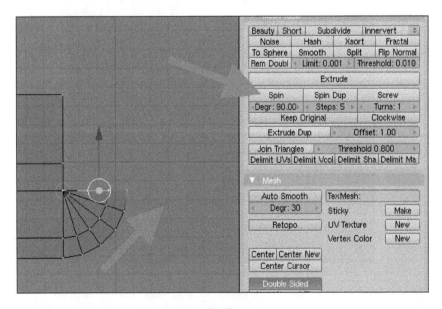

With a spin of 90 degrees, 5 steps, and the copies made in a counterclockwise direction, the resulting model will look like the image below shows. It's still not finished yet; we have to close the upper part of the model. Select the edges pointed in the following figure and extrude them twice to close the model. To make the placement of the vertices a lot easier, we can use the vertex snapping discussed in the previous chapter.

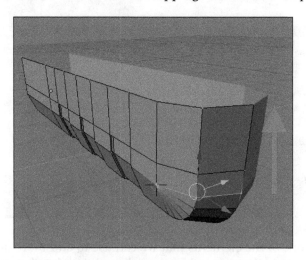

Adding creases and rounded details

Now it's time to add some creases and ornaments to the model by using a very common loop cut technique. First, add two new loops to the model, making sure that those new loops are really close to each other. Another way to create two edge loops close to each other is by creating only a single loop first by using the *Ctrl+R* keys. After creating this loop, hold down the *Alt* key and right-click on any edge of the loop to select the complete edge loop. When the loop is selected, press the *W* key and choose **Bevel** to split the loop into two.

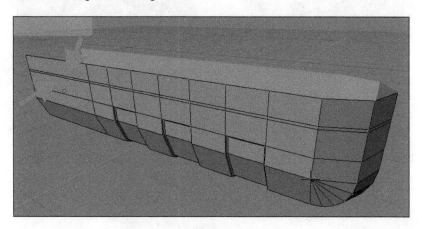

The model will now have a lot of narrow faces, which we will be selecting next. Right after the selection of those faces, extrude them twice, more toward the interior of the model. Since the final model will have a subsurf modifier applied, it's important to make two extrusions for the crease:

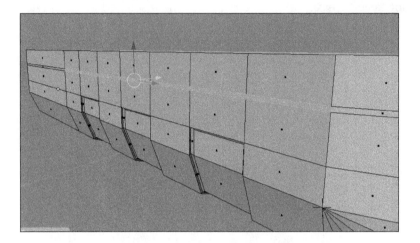

The crease is just one of the elements that we can use to add more details to a model; another important tool allows us to blend small rounded details to objects. At this point, we have to be careful to not mess up the topology of the model.

That's why we have to add a mesh circle and blend it to the model.

In order to add a circle to the model and build details resembling a button or switch in the gun, we must first create a few more loops. Using the *Ctrl+R* shortcut keys, add four extra loops to the model.

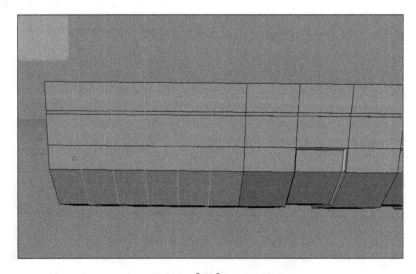

Change the work mode to faces, and select only the four faces shown in the following figure. We will then erase these faces and end up with a hole in the mesh.

To create the circle in the right position, we have to first place the 3D cursor in the middle of the hole. Select all eight vertices of the hole, and with the snap option, move the 3D cursor to the center of the hole.

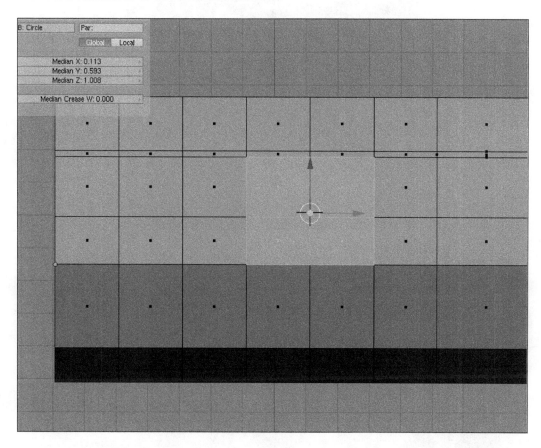

When the cursor is placed, create a mesh circle with eight vertices, as illustrated in the following image. To connect the circle to the rest of the mesh, we will select four vertices that delimitate a face and press the *F* key to create a new face. Repeat the process eight times until the circle is connected to the mesh.

In Blender 3D we have an option called **Auto fill**, which can automatically fill any set of selected vertices with faces. To use this option, just press the *Shift+F* keys with more than two vertices selected. This method may seem faster, but its downside is that it creates triangular faces. In polygon modeling, the use of triangular faces is always problematic because it doesn't form a regular set of edge loops, which can hinder the editing process of the edges later.

To reorganize the faces, press *Ctrl+Shift+F*. Doing this, however, will not remove the triangular faces.

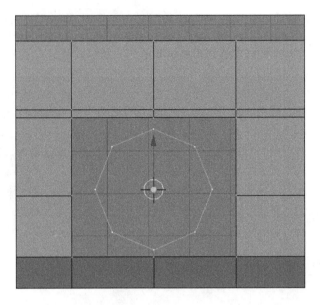

With the circle connected to the mesh, we can work on the edges pointed in the following image:

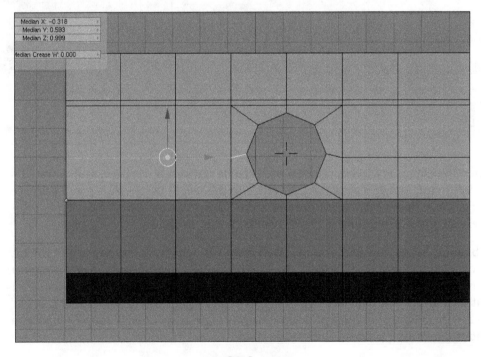

Select those edges and press the *W* key to access the specials menu. Then, choose the bevel option to split these edges into two. This will create new faces connected to the circle. Select all of the objects in the model, and press the *W* key again to choose the **Remove doubles** option to remove any extra vertex.

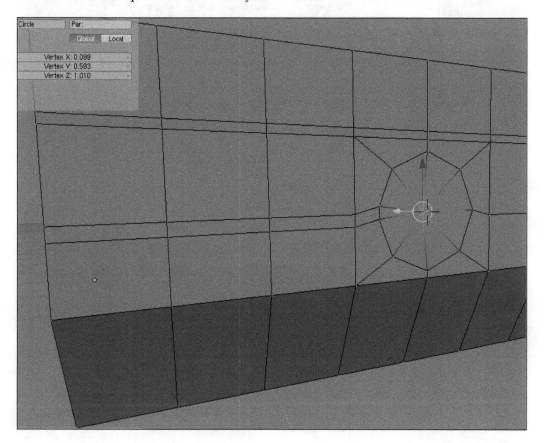

The objective of the next extrusion is to create a kind of crease that connects to the circle and makes it a bit more interesting. To do that, we have to select the faces pointed in the following image:

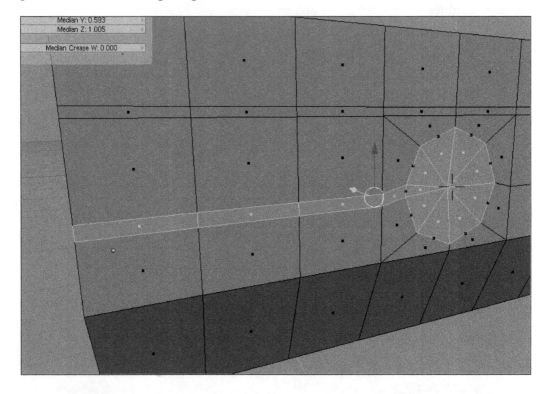

After selecting the faces, extrude them more toward the inside of the model. That will be enough for the crease, but the circle still needs some work. So, select only the faces in the interior of the circle.

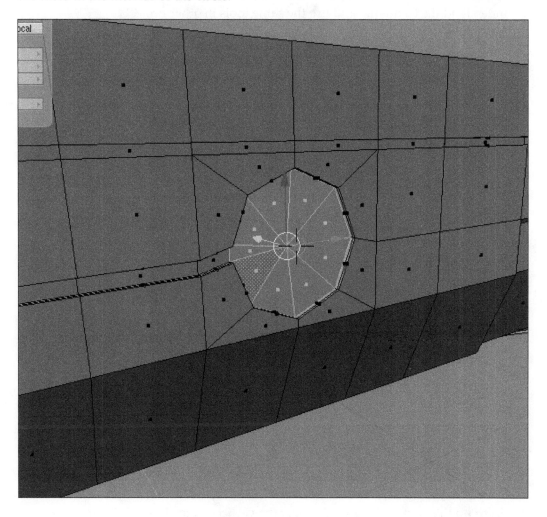

To create the details for this circle, use a sequence of extrudes and scales to create a structure that looks like the next figure. The number and size of the structure can change according to your vision of the project. The important part of the project is to understand the technique and use the same tools in other projects.

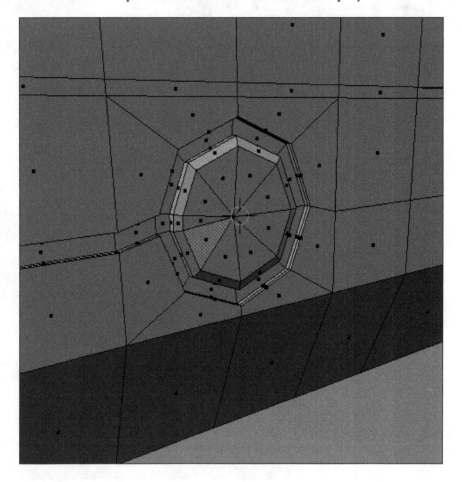

To finish up this part of the project, select the vertices in the lower-left part of the model and move them up. It will create a new plane and give even more importance to the place where the shooter will hold the weapon.

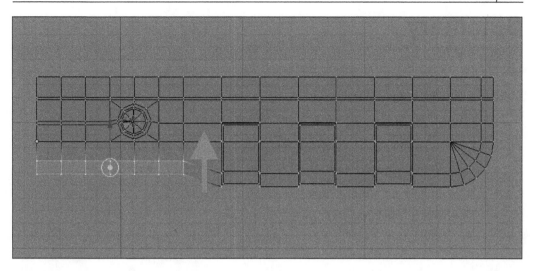

This is what the model looks like, placed together with the rest of the base model created in the previous chapter:

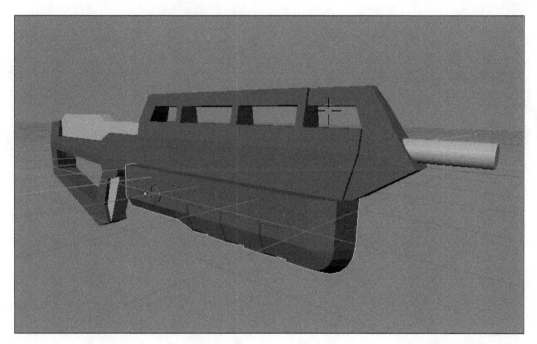

This part of the model is done! In the next chapter, we will continue working on the model, adding details by using textures and displacement maps to create small modifications to the mesh, using only images.

Summary

In this chapter, we learned more about poly modeling with Blender. We also learned about new tools, such as snapping, released a few months ago.

Here is a list of what we learned:

- How to create creases
- How to use Blender's new snapping tools
- How to use the spin tool
- How to add a circular shape to a mesh
- How to use the bevel tool

5
Rendering the Project with YafaRay

With the modeling complete and only a few parts left out, our first Incredible Machine is almost done. In this case, the missing parts are related to the final render of the image and the addition of an environment to present the object.

In this chapter, we will finish the weapon project with the setup of textures and materials for the model and the installation and setup of an external render engine for Blender 3D. The render engine for this project will be YafaRay, which allows us to use advanced global illumination features not available in the Blender internal render. For this project in particular, we will learn how to install and use the renderer to use it in more detail during the next project.

YafaRay renderer

The YafaRay renderer is very famous among Blender artists and is by far one of the best tools to work side-by-side with Blender. For a long time, we had a direct link from the Blender user interface to render scenes and projects with YafaRay. In the past few months, the renderer suffered a complete rewrite, and a huge upgrade was made in order to make YafaRay even better and to add more features such as different render methods and capabilities. As YafaRay is open source software, just like Blender, we can download and install it free of cost on any computer, with versions available for Windows, Linux, and Mac OS X.

To download the latest version of YafaRay, just visit the official YafaRay website at http://www.yafaray.org, and look for a version compatible with your operational system. For this project, we will be using version 0.1.1, which is the most updated version available at the time of writing.

In order to use YafaRay, we have to install Python because all of the integration from Blender 3D to YafaRay is made by an exporter script that converts all of the Blender scenes to a format readable by YafaRay. All scripts in Blender use a language called Python, and if Python is not installed, the exporter won't work. To download Python, visit http://www.python.org. For Blender 2.49, we have to use Python 2.6.X.

Installing YafaRay

When both Python and YafaRay installers are downloaded, we can begin installing them. Install Python before YafaRay and choose all of the default options. The next step is to install YafaRay; just choose the default options and it will be installed. To check if the renderer is correctly installed, open Blender 3D and you will find the export option in the Render menu of the scripts window.

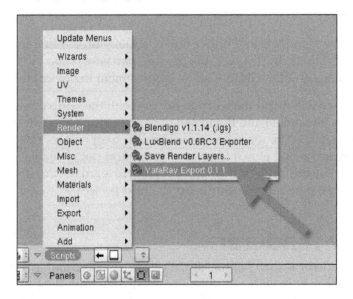

This is a script placed automatically by the YafaRay installer and should appear after the installation process. If the option doesn't appear, something happened during the installation process making the exporter unavailable.

The first problem may be that a previous version of YafaRay is already be installed on your machine before an update. To avoid problems, it's recommended that you uninstall the previous versions of YafaRay and manually erase any versions of the exporter script in the Blender scripts folder.

Another problem is that you might encounter is an error message when the exporter script is called.

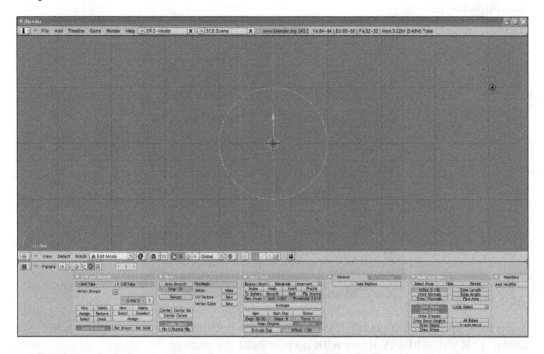

This occurs when Python is not installed when the YafaRay export script is executed. To fix this error, try to install Python again.

Creating a studio environment

With YafaRay and Python installed, we can begin working on the environment for the weapon. When the objective of the project is to show an object like our Incredible Machine, one of the best environments to use is a *Studio Setup*. It works much like a photography studio with an infinite background and a light setup that shows most of the object and reflective parts. The modeling of a scene like this is quite simple, and it only requires a bended plane that will work as the background of the studio. Before anything, place the weapon models into a separated layer to avoid any confusion with the modeling.

There are several ways to add the plane to the scene, and the easiest one is made with a mesh cylinder. Add a mesh cylinder to the scene, as shown in the following image:

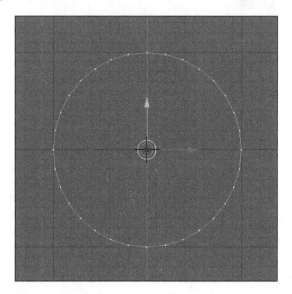

Turn the **Cap Ends** button off. It is located at the bottom of the cylinder creation menu. This will add a cylinder with no planes at the ends of the object.

In edit mode, select only a quarter of the cylinder, and using the *W* key, choose **Select Swap**.

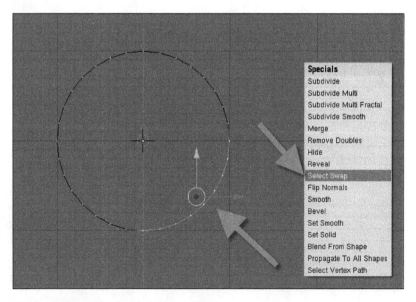

This will invert the selection of the vertices. The objective is to leave only a quarter of the cylinder and erase all other vertices like the following image shows. When the vertices are selected, press the *X* key and choose **Vertices** to erase all of the remaining vertices.

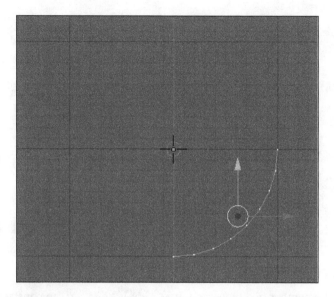

With the model still in edit mode, select one edge of the cylinder, as shown in the following image:

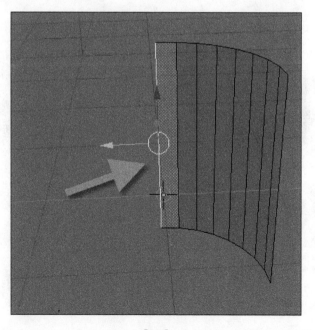

With the extrude tool, create two new faces.

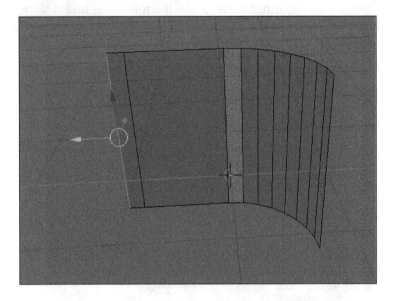

Constraining the extrude

Remember that by using the X, Y, or Z keys, we can constrain the extrusion to a single axis. In the preceding image, the extrusion was created with a constraint to the Y axis.

Repeat the same process for the other side of the mesh cylinder.

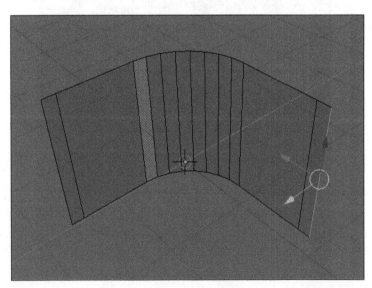

To finish the background of the studio, rotate the model and align it to the grid as shown in the following screenshot. Change the work mode to object, and use the *R* key to rotate the model 90 degrees. Next, press the *X* key to constrain the rotation to the X axis. Hold down the *Ctrl* key while the model is being rotated to snap the rotation to the grid.

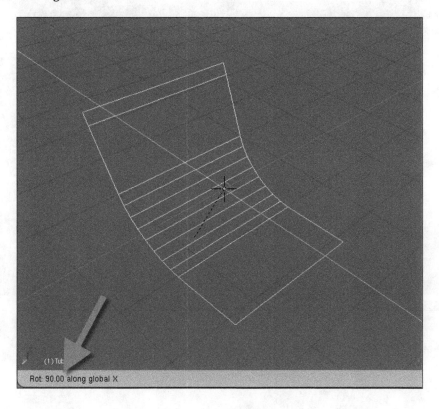

When the model is rotated, adjust its scale by using the *S* key, and constrain the transformation to the *Y* axis by using the *Y* key. To finish editing the background, press the **Set Smooth** button and add a **Subsurf** modifier to the model.

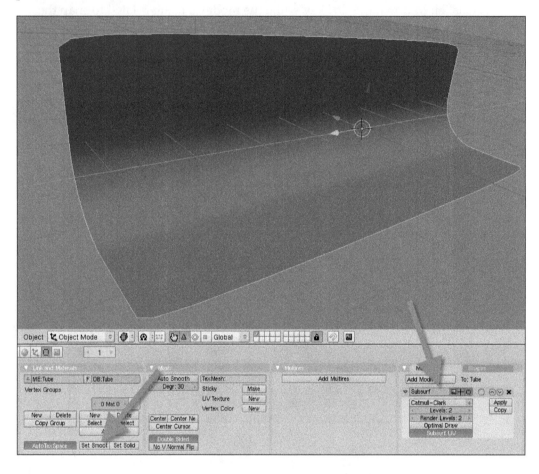

The next step is to add a cube around the studio background to control the illumination that we will be using for the scene. Add a mesh cube, and scale until it surrounds the background that we just created.

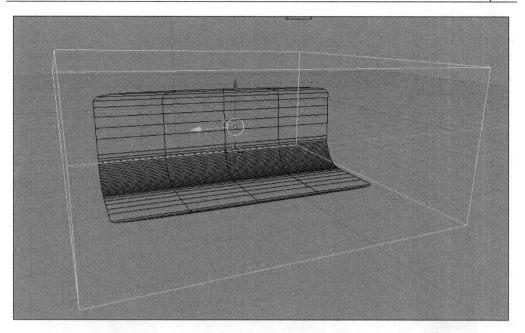

Adding light to the scene

For this scene, we will use two area lights to simulate the overall light of a real studio. This is a common technique used to light up those environments with a set of spots organized as a plane of light. We can create an **Area** lamp in Blender with the **Lamp** option in the toolbox.

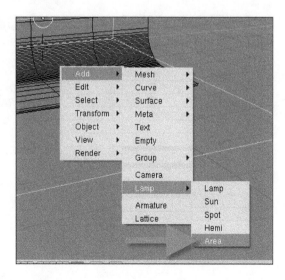

When the **Area** lamp is created, it will be pointing down. With the rotate transformation, change the orientation of the lamp and make it parallel to the X or Y axis. The **Area** lamp must be placed on the side of the background we just created.

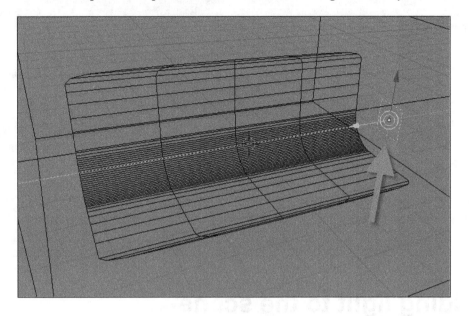

As the **Area** lamp is too small, we have to make it bigger. With the **Area** lamp, we have to always change the size of the lamp at the shading panel, which can be opened by using the *F5* key. There we will find the **Size** option to change the size of the lamp.

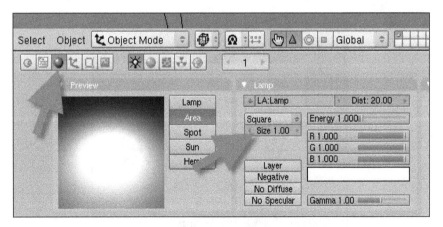

Increase the size of the lamp until it looks like following image. For this image, the size of 5 units was used.

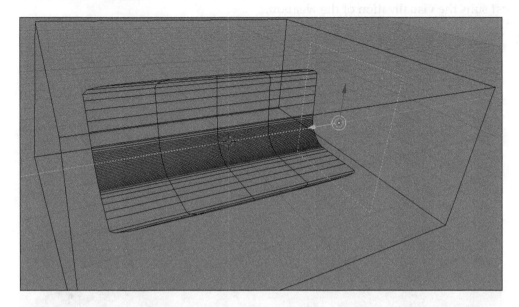

The last step is to duplicate the lamp using the *Shift+D* keys when the object is selected, and rotate it in a way that the lamp will point in the opposite direction.

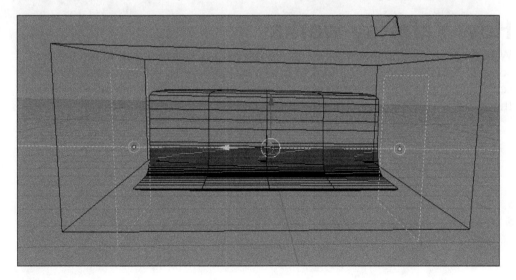

With the scene ready, we can turn on the visibility of the layers where our weapon model is placed. Place it as shown in the following image, or find another angle that best suits the visualization of the weapon.

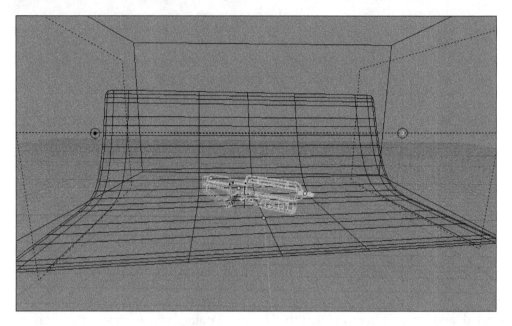

How YafaRay works

With the textures and materials setup completed, we can move on to render the scene in YafaRay. Let's take a look at how YafaRay works. When we call the export script, a few tabs will appear to set up the working of render. Each tab will control the scene in a certain way, from the object settings to the render method.

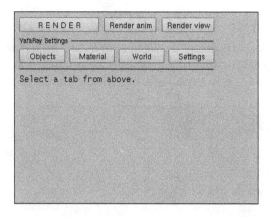

There are four tabs available:

1. **Objects**: This tab controls aspects of each object, such as the ability to emit light or different types of cameras or lights. The options change based on the type of object that is selected. For instance, if a camera is selected, we will see options to edit the camera, and a lamp will show options to control the way it will light the scene in YafaRay.

2. **Material**: The name of this tab is self-explanatory; it controls the materials in the scene. There are several types of materials to choose from.

3. **World**: A scene in YafaRay may have a lot of different aspects that we could change. In this tab, we can choose the background color, background settings, and even add a simulation of a SunSky.

4. **Settings**: Among all the tabs, this is one of the most important because it controls the method used to render the scene. The render method can be decisive to control the quality and amount of time required to generate the images.

With the **RENDER** button, we will start the rendering process of a still image, and the **Render anim** will call all frames from an animation.

For this project, we have to change the materials of the objects, light types, and set the render method for the scene.

Setting lights in YafaRay

To control lights in YafaRay, select the light source and go to the **Objects** tab. There we will find a contextual menu that shows options related to an object based on its nature. For instance, if we select the **Area Lights**, these will be the options displayed:

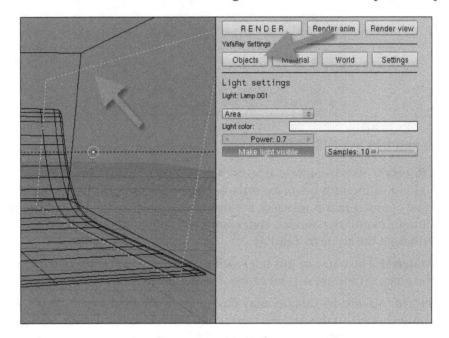

Select each lamp and change the settings to the following:

- Type: Area
- Power: 0.7
- Make light visible: On
- Samples: 10
- Color: White

This will set the light as **Area Lamp** recognized by YafaRay with an intensity of 0.7 units. The samples setting will add more quality to the soft shadows created by the lamp. In the end, we will have the color of the light, which will be white to create a clean and bright light environment for the studio. Apply the same settings to both lamps.

Adding materials to the weapon

In YafaRay, we can control materials with a proper tab called **Material**. To be able to control materials there, we have to add a material to each object in the **Blender Shading** panel. Just add a material to an object, and we will override it in the YafaRay tab. In our scene, we will use four materials divided into these base colors:

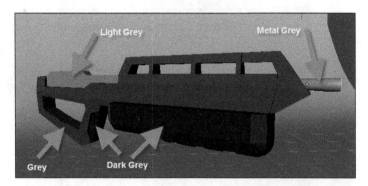

Select an object and add a material to it using the **Add New** button.

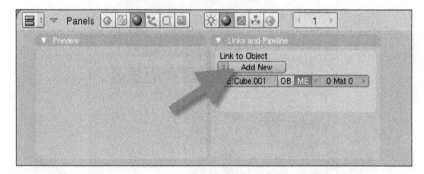

When the material is added, change the name of the material to make it easier to find in the YafaRay tab.

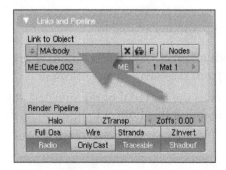

Repeat the same process for all objects, and give them unique and easy-to-remember names. Now, we can go to the **Material** tab of YafaRay.

There we will find all options related to the management of the materials.

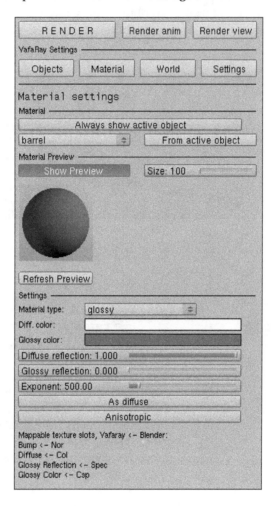

Here are descriptions of the options available:

- **Always show active object**: When this button is pressed, we are only able to edit the material from the active object selected.

- **From active object**: If the material of the selected object is not showing up in the **Material** tab, press this button to update the display of the selected object material.

- **Refresh Preview/Show Preview**: This option displays a preview of the material, and the **Refresh** button shows the changes made in the settings of a material on the preview window.

- **Material type**: Here, we find the selector where we pick each material type for the object.

For all objects in the scene, we will use a **glossy** material with the default settings, making changes only to the material color. The changes made to these settings are the ones that will be displayed in the rendering.

To change the color of the material, use the **Diff. color** option:

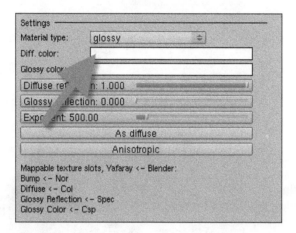

Framing the weapon

The last step before we begin working on the rendering settings is to adjust the framing of the weapon. Just like in the Blender internal render engine, in YafaRay we can only render what the camera sees. Place the view of the model as shown in the following screenshot and press *Ctrl+Alt+0* to adjust the framing of the camera.

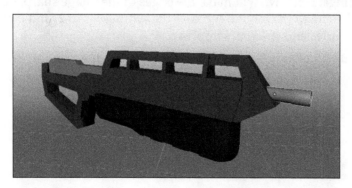

Final render with YafaRay

With everything set and ready, we can go to the **Settings** tab of YafaRay and choose
how the image will be rendered. In YafaRay, we have several types of methods
that we can use for rendering, but for this project, we will use one of the simplest
methods called **Direct Illumination**. We will only change the settings pointed out
in the following screenshot:

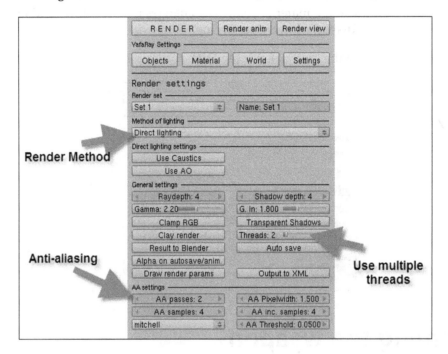

- **Render Method**: Pick a method called **Direct lighting** to use a simple way
  to light the scene. This is a good choice as we are using area lights to spread
  light energy.

- **A settings**: Here, we will make the edges of the image sharper and add
  anti-aliasing to the render. Increase the **AA passes** to **2**, and increase
  AA samples and **AA inc. samples** to **4**.

- **Threads**: Choose how many threads you want to use in the rendering.

To control the render size, we use the controls available in the **Scene** panel of Blender:

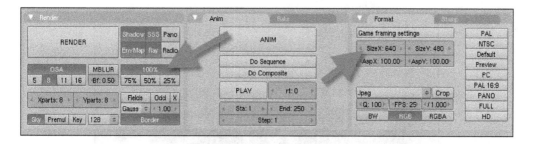

When the YafaRay **RENDER** button is pressed, a new window will appear showing our image being rendered. There we will find an option to save the project as an image:

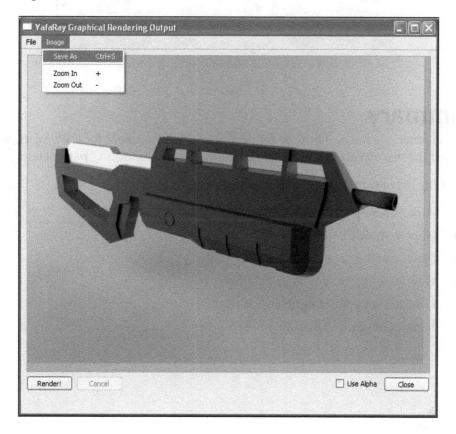

That's it! Our first project is finished. In the next projects, we will continue to use more options in YafaRay and learn a lot more of the advanced render features.

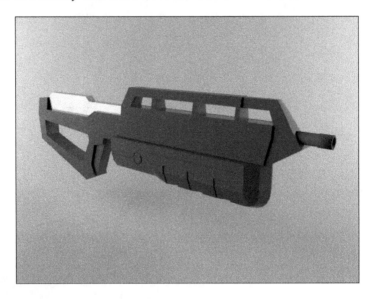

Summary

In this chapter, we learned how to set up the final environment for the project, which involved the use of YafaRay with special materials and rendering parameters.

Here is the list of things that we have learned in this chapter:

- How to set up a studio environment
- How to install YafaRay
- How to export a scene to YafaRay
- How to set up materials in YafaRay
- How to set up basic lights in YafaRay
- How to render in YafaRay

6
Steampunk Spacecraft

In the previous project, creating a hand weapon was a great introduction to the modeling techniques required to continuously increase the difficulty level of your projects. It's time to start working on our second Incredible Machine, and for this second project we will be manipulating a bigger object. The main objective for this second part of the book is to create a steampunk spacecraft with even smaller details and more UV mapping techniques to add more realism to the model.

Steampunk concept

Before we actually begin working on the model, let's make clear the difference between a regular spacecraft and a steampunk spacecraft. Although both of them are based on science fiction, the steampunk spacecraft has a few important characteristics that differ from a regular hi-tech spacecraft.

Imagine a world where the advances of science and machinery were actually developed centuries ago. For example, imagine medieval knights using hi-tech armor and destroying castles with rockets. It may sound strange, as the rockets have been made only for the army in the last century. What would a fighter jet look like in the Middle Ages? It would be a mix of steel, glass, and wood.

The steampunk environment is made out of these kinds of things, modern objects and vehicles produced and developed in a parallel universe, where those discoveries were made long ago.

The secret of designing a good steampunk vehicle or object is to mix the recent technology with the materials and methods available in past times, such as wood and bronze to make a space suit. If you need some inspiration to design objects like those, watch some recent movies that use a steampunk environment to create some interesting machines. But, to really get to the source, I do recommend that you read some books written by Jules Verne, who wrote about incredible environments and machines that dive deep into the ocean or travel to outer space.

The following image is an example of a steampunk weapon (Image credits: Halogen Gallery, licensed under Creative Commons):

Next is a steampunk historical character (Image credits: Sparr0, licensed under Creative Commons):

Here are a few resources to find out more about Steampunk:

- Steampunk at Wikipedia, with lots of resources:
  http://en.wikipedia.org/wiki/Steampunk

- Guide to drawing and creating steampunk machinery:
  http://www.crabfu.com/steamtoys/diy_steampunk/
- Showcase of steampunk technology:
  http://www.instructables.com/id/Steampunk/

Spacecraft concept

Now that we know how to design a good steampunk machine, let's discuss the concept of this spacecraft. For this project, we will design a machine that mixes some elements of steel, but not those fancy industrial plates and welded parts. Instead, our machine will have the look and feel of a machine built by a blacksmith. As it would be really strange to have wooden parts for a spacecraft, we will skip or use this material only for the interior.

Other aspects of the machine that will help give the impression of a steampunk spacecraft are as follows:

- Riveted sheets of metal
- Metal with the look of bronze
- Valves and pipes

With that in mind, we can start with this concept image to create our spacecraft:

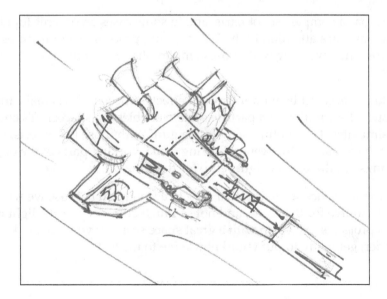

It's not a complete project, but we're off to a great start with Blender and our use of polygons to create the basis for this Incredible Machine.

Project workflow

This project will improve our modeling and creating skills with Blender to a great extent! So, to make the process more efficient, the workflow will be planned as this would be done by a professional studio. This is the best way to optimize the time and quality of the project. It will also guarantee that future projects will be finished in the shortest timeframe.

The first step for all projects is to find some reference images or photos for the pre-visualization stage. At this point, we should make all important decisions about a project based only on your concept studies. The biggest amount of time spent on this type of project is with artistic decisions like the framing of the camera, type and color of materials, shape of the object, and environment setup.

All of those decisions should be made before we open Blender and start modeling because a simple detour on the main concept could result in a partial or total loss of all work.

When all of the decisions are made, the next step is to start modeling with the reference images we found on the Internet, or we can draw the references ourselves. The modeling stage involves the spacecraft and the related environment, which of course will be outer space. For this environment, Blender will help us design a space with nebulas, star fields, and even a glazing star. Right after the environment is finished, we will begin working with some materials and textures.

As the object has a complex set of parts, and in some cases an organic topology, we will have to pay extra attention to the UV mapping process to add textures. We'll use a few tips when working with those complex shapes and topology to simplify the process.

What would a spacecraft be without special effects? Special effects make the project more realistic. The addition of a particle system enables the spacecraft's engines to work and simulates the shooting of a plasma gun. With those two effects, we will be able to give dynamism to the scene, showing some working parts of the object. And, to finish things up, there is the light setup for the scene.

A light setup for a space scene is rather easy to accomplish because we will only have a strong light source for the scene, and not so much bouncing for the light rays. The goal for this project is to end up with a great space scene. If you already know how to use Blender, get ready to put your knowledge to the test!

Building edges and planes for the spacecraft

The technique used to build this model is called edge modeling or poly modeling, which is a derivation of subdivision. In this type of modeling, we have to progressively create edges and faces to build the overall model, which will result in creating a full model. Even if it seems difficult and hard to complete, we have full control over the topology of the model with this type of modeling. It is very important to have control over the topology for models like machines, where the precision and organization of the vertices, edges, and faces can really matter.

The other important aspect of the project, if we look at the concept images, is the fact that this object is perfectly symmetrical, so we can build only half of the spacecraft and mirror the other part.

Creating the first section of the spacecraft

Open Blender and start a new model in top view, adding a mesh cube to the scene. This will be the object used to derive all other geometry for this first step of the spacecraft.

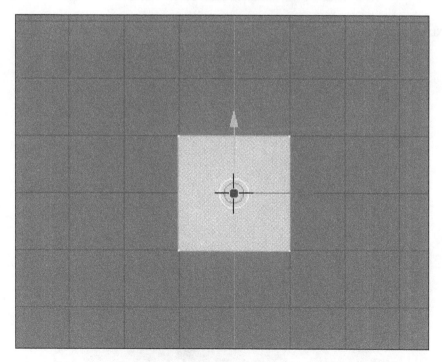

While in edit mode, select the bottom edge of the plane and with the *E* key extrude it four times.

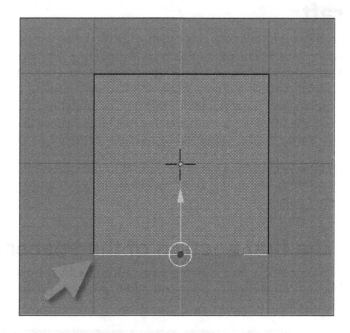

The extrusions should follow the proportions shown in the following image:

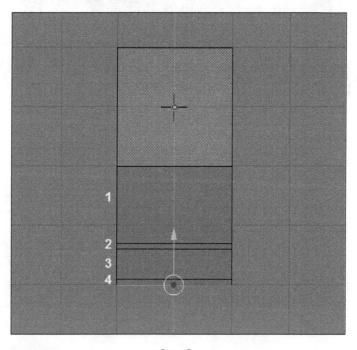

The next step is to rotate the view. Without rotating the model with the middle mouse button, select only the faces pointed out in the following image:

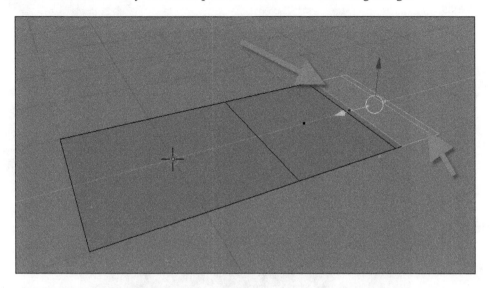

Then, move them just a bit along the Z axis.

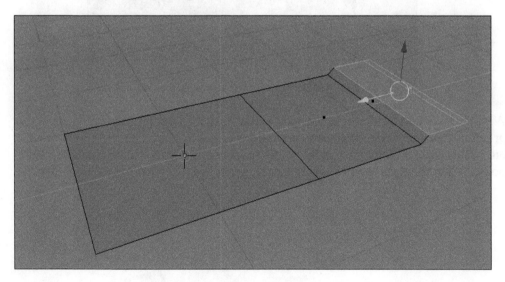

Change the selection mode to edge with the *Ctrl+Tab* keys, and choose the edges on the lower right side of the model. There, we will extrude the edges down the Z axis.

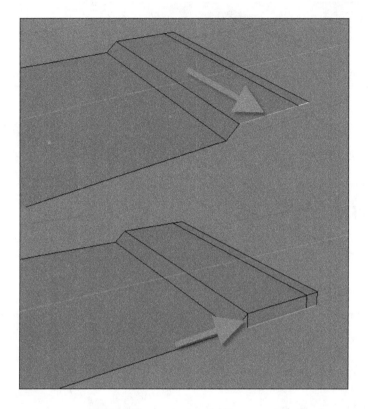

With the selection mode set to vertices, select only the small triangle created in the previous extrude. Triangular faces are harder to control and can mess up a mesh, but in this case, it won't be a problem because no edge loop will be created at that point. When the three vertices are selected, press the *F* key to create a new face.

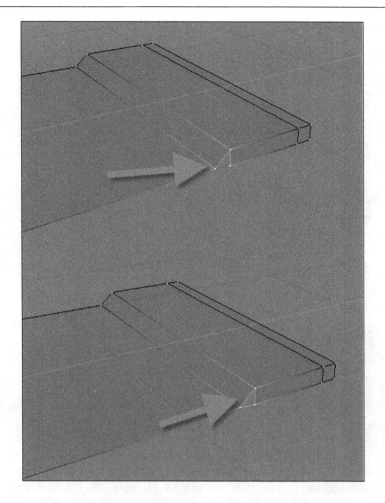

Now, we can begin creating the side part of the model that will connect down with the wing. Select the edges pointed out in the following image:

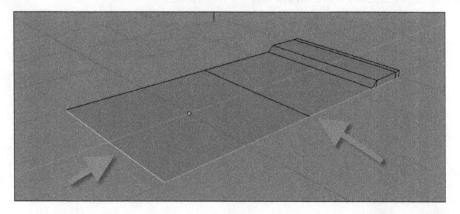

Then, extrude the edges four times in the Z direction.

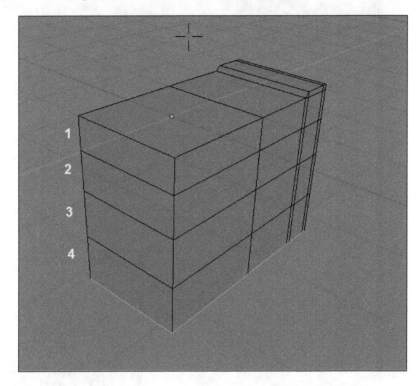

Because a big part of the main body is beginning to appear, we can start making a few adjustments to the last extruded edges. Those edges are pointed out in the following image. To make the selection easier, just hold down the *Alt* key and click on one edge to select the full loop. If any extra edge gets into the selection, just click on it with the *Shift* key pressed to remove the edge from the selection. Each loop must be selected individually and moved a bit to the right along the X axis. This will create a small curvature on the side of the model.

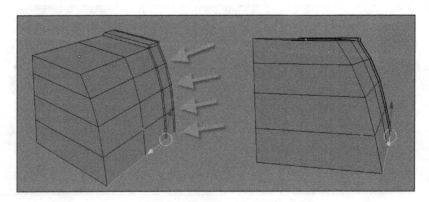

Repeat the same process for the edges at the back of the model.

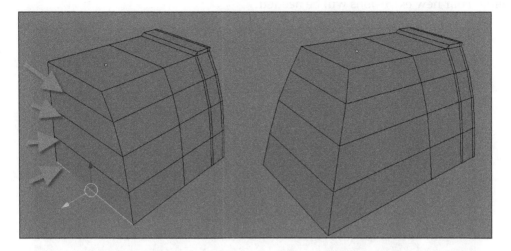

Modeling the wing

With the first part of the modeling created, we can now work on the wing modeling. The wing will be created from a series of extrusions coming from the side of the model, and the edges that we must select are pointed out in the following image:

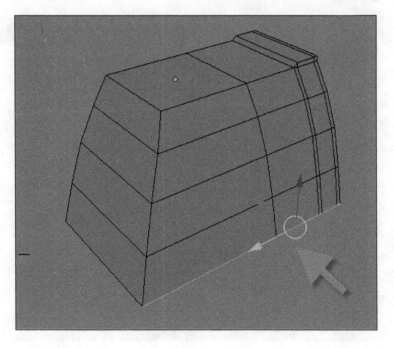

Set the view to top and start a series of extrusions to create the mesh required for the wing. Four new extrusions will be needed.

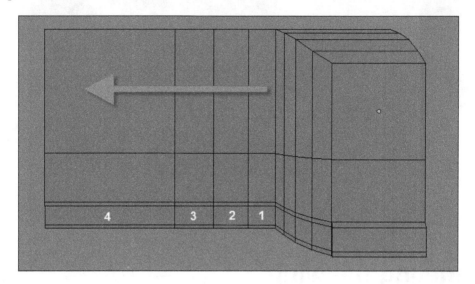

With the base for the wing created, we will move a few vertices to shape the wing. Change the work mode to vertex, and move the vertices pointed out in the following image:

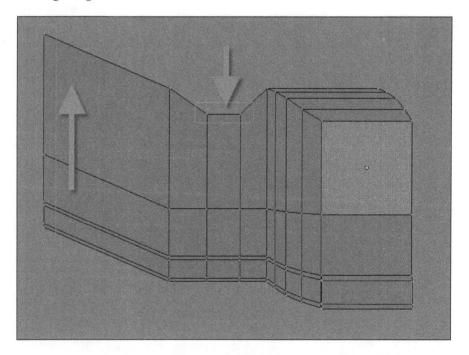

Those vertices were moved down in the Y axis.

Rotate the view to select the edges pointed out in the following image, and move them up in the Z axis. It will simulate a turbine air entry.

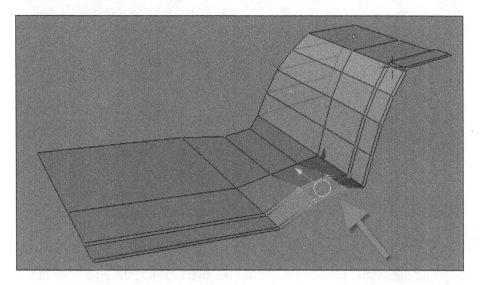

Modeling the front

The basis for the wing is created, so now we can move forward to the front of the spacecraft. To start modeling the front, select two edges located on the side of the wing, as shown in the following image:

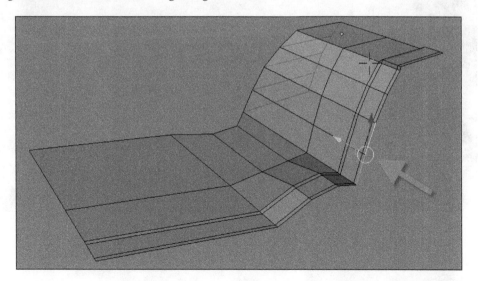

With those vertices selected, extrude them three times.

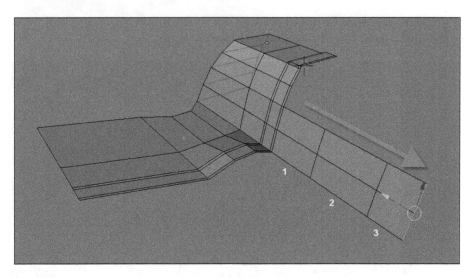

If you have not yet saved the project, now would be a good time to do so.

To finish this part of the project, select only the two edges at the right side of the model, and extrude them along the X axis.

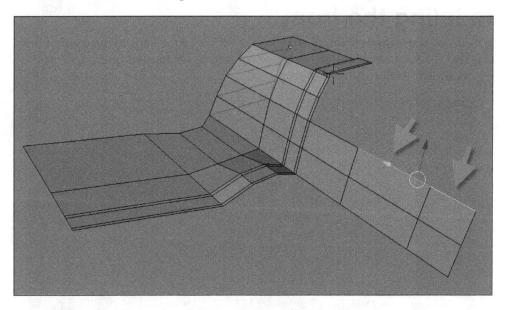

This will be the basis for the modeling of the cockpit.

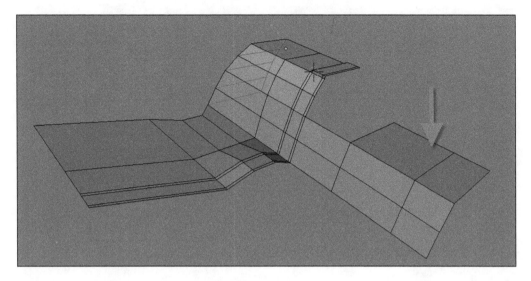

Summary

In this chapter, we learned more about our second Incredible Machine. Our first step was to create a base mesh for the spacecraft, which will be detailed and improved in the next chapters. So far, we've used edge modeling, deforming, and we've adjusted the shape of a model to get the shape of the object.

Here is a brief summary of what we have learned:

- The definition of steampunk
- The characteristics of a steampunk machine
- How to contextualize a steampunk machine
- What the project will look like
- An overview of the workflow for a professional project
- How edge modeling works
- How to create a model from a single face
- How to shape the model by transforming edges, vertices, and faces

7
Working with Smaller Areas

In the previous chapter, we started our second Incredible Machine project—a steampunk spacecraft. The base mesh of the machine was created in the last chapter, and now we can move forward, adding more details and parts to the model. You'll notice in this chapter that most of the modeling process is a repetition of small tasks necessary to create the full model.

Modeling the front of the spacecraft

First, we will work on the front of the model, starting where we left off in the last chapter. For almost the entire model, we will use the edge modeling technique to create the spacecraft for better control of the topology of the model. If you don't remember the basis for this technique, all we have to do is select an element of the mesh, such as a vertex, edge, or face, with the extrude tool and create new parts of the model. In this project, the snapping tools of Blender will be very important to build the model with the minimum of precision.

Take the model finished in the last chapter, and in the edit mode, select the edge pointed in the following image:

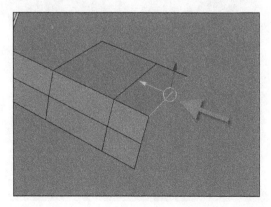

With the edge selected, press the *E* key to create an extrusion. Right after the extrusion, move the new edge down a bit. When the new edge is placed, press the *E* key again to create another extrusion and move it down as well, until the new faces look like the ones displayed in the following image:

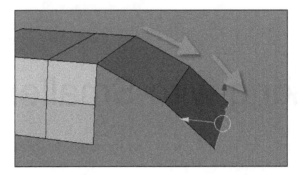

With the front part created, we can now select a few vertices of the model to create two faces and close the model on the side. Change the selection mode to vertex, and select the three vertices pointed in the following screenshot. When all three vertices are selected, press the *F* key and a face will be created.

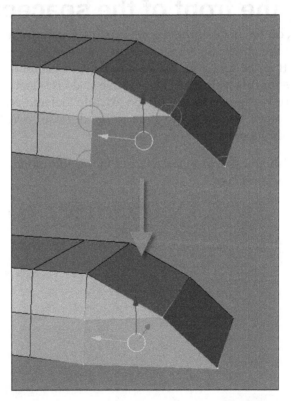

Repeat the same operation with the following four vertices:

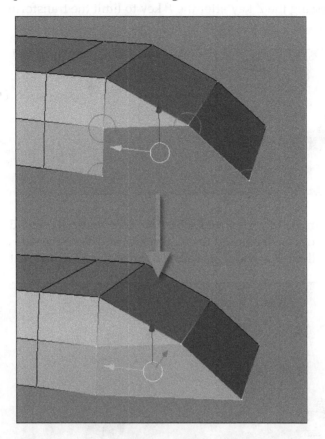

Now that the front part of the spacecraft is closed, we can add the edges and faces required to close the bottom of the model. To do that, rotate the view and select the edge pointed in the following screenshot:

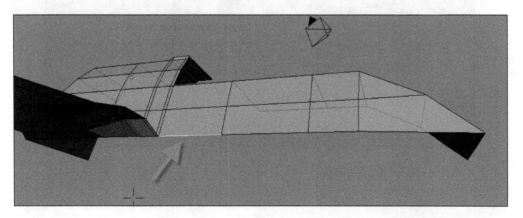

Press the *E* key and extrude this face just a bit down in the Z axis. This can be achieved by pressing the *Z* key after the *E* key to limit the transformation to the Z axis.

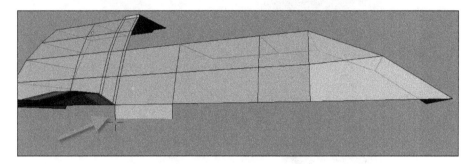

Set the selection mode to vertex, and select the three vertices pointed in the following image. Those vertices will be used to create a face and close the side of the spacecraft's fuselage. When all three vertices are selected, press the *F* key to create a face.

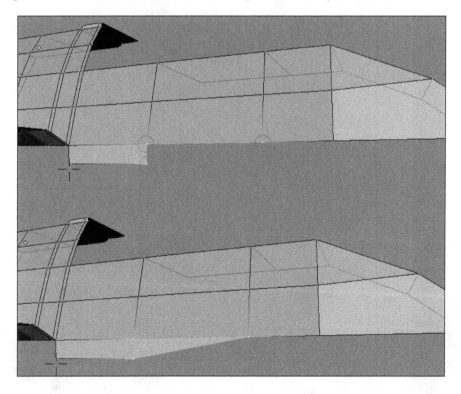

Now, we can create the faces at the bottom of the cockpit. We will use the edges pointed in the following image. The creation of the edges at the front are crucial for this task because we will use them with the snap tool to better position the faces at the bottom of the cockpit.

Here is how it will work:

1. Turn the snap tool of Blender on and leave it snapping to the closest vertices.

2. Select and extrude the edges while holding down the *Ctrl* key.

3. Move the mouse cursor near the desired vertices, and they will snap to the vertices.

Let's apply this sequence to our project, and to do that, we have to select the edges pointed in the following image. Turn the snapping tool of Blender on.

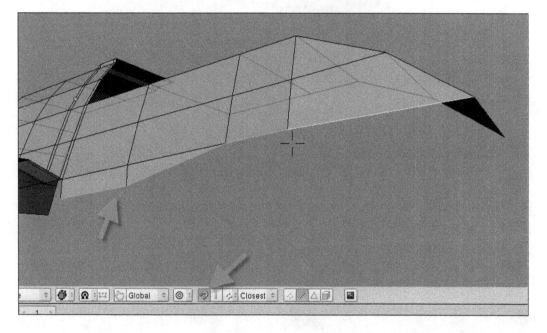

Press the *E* key to extrude the edges, and hold down the *Ctrl* key. Move the cursor near the middle-front vertex of the model, and a small white circle will show the snap position.

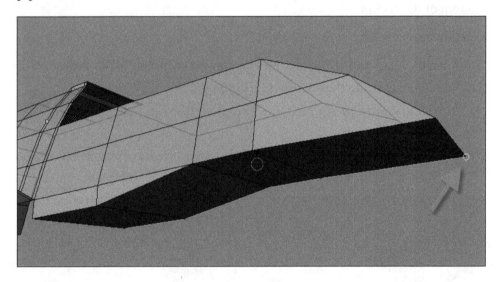

Adding details to the wing

With the cockpit created, we can move to the wing and add the final details and geometry to finish the model. To create the full wing, we will use the mirror tool in Blender, which is different from the mirror modifier used later in the chapter. Besides the mirror, all of the tools used are the transformation options, such as move, rotate, and scale, along with the extrude.

The first step required is changing the view to front. This can be done by pressing the *1* key on the numeric keyboard. Set the view mode to wireframe with the *Z* key, and select all faces of the wing:

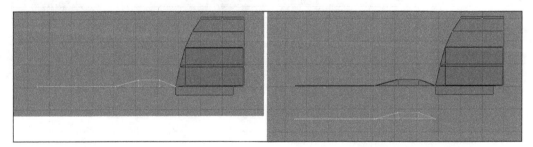

Before we mirror the object, press the *Shift+D* keys to duplicate the wing model and place the copy below the original model, like the right side of the previous image.

While the copied wing is still selected, press the *Ctrl+M* keys to mirror the model. The mirror tool can invert the position of an object based on one axis. Right after the mirror tool, we must press the X, Y, or Z keys to select an axis for the mirror. For this model, the axis used in the mirror is Z.

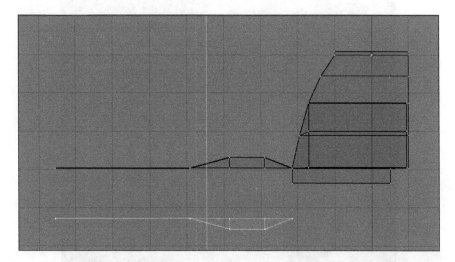

When the model is mirrored and placed, we must connect the new faces to the rest of the model. To do that, rotate the view to see the model as shown in the following image. With the snap tool turned on, move the object until it snaps to the vertex pointed in the following image:

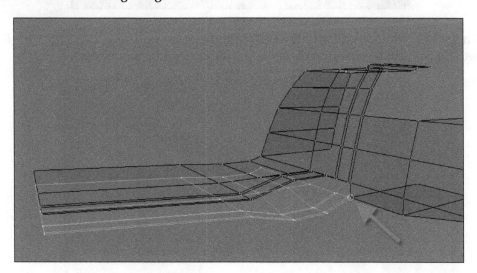

In this last creation, the wing parts were created and placed near each other, but we still have to close and connect the edges around the wing. This step is simple to accomplish. All we have to do is select two edges and connect them with a new face with the *F* key. Select the two edges pointed in the next screenshot and press the *F* key:

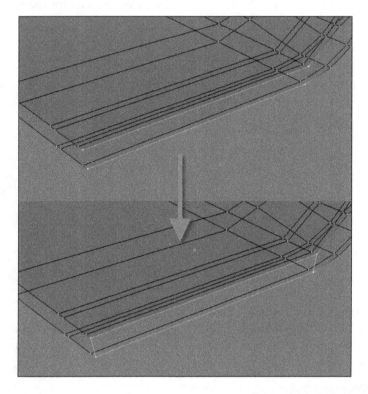

With the loop cut tool, add an edge at the middle of the new face. Press the *Ctrl+R* keys, and confirm the creation of the loop with the middle mouse button.

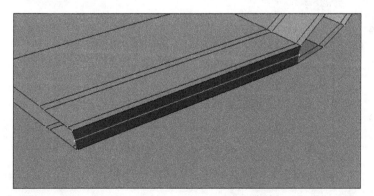

To finish up the front of the wing, move the new edge forward.

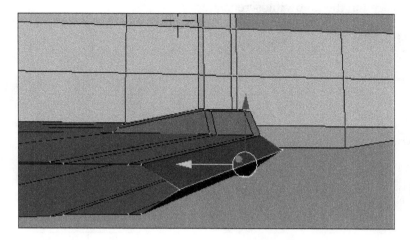

Modeling the engines

At the front and back of the wing, we have an engine blended to the wing shape, which must be modeled. This will involve the creation of a few planes and edges just like the other parts of the spacecraft, but with more attention to the small areas. Rotate the view until we see the front part of the engine's air entrance, and select the three vertices pointed in the following image:

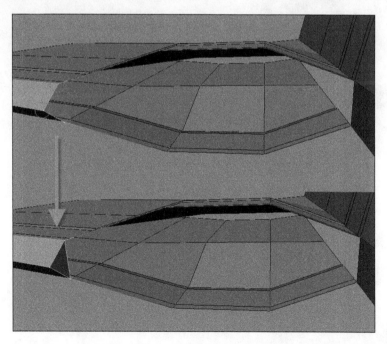

Repeat the same process to create the next face on the right, selecting four vertices this time as seen in the following screenshot:

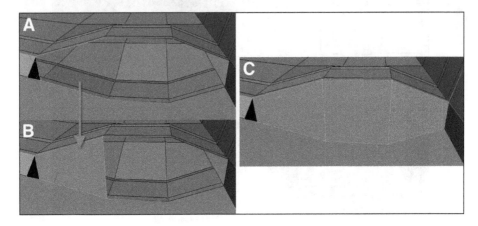

We will now create a few faces with a combination of extrusions and scale transformations. To begin, we must select all faces of the engine's air entrance, like the previous figure shows. Press the *E* key and press the *Esc* key to cancel the extrusion. This will create the new faces, but it won't place them anywhere. Press the *S* key and scale the faces:

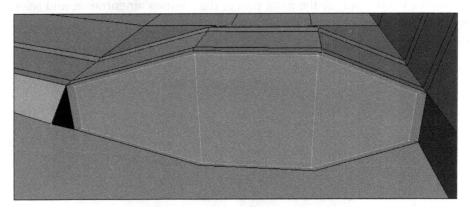

Repeat the same process four more times until we get a structure similar to the one in the next screenshot:

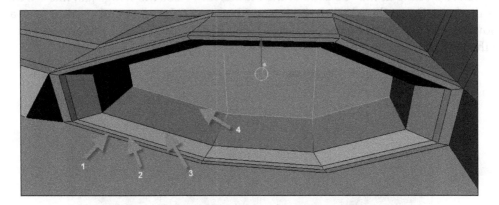

From these four extrusions, we will use a combination of extrusions and scale in all of them. However, in the second, third, and fourth extrusions, we will also move the edges back some. This will finish the creation of the engine's air entrance.

Now, we can turn our attention to the back of the wing and create the backside of the engine just like we did for the front. First, rotate the view to see the back of the engine, and select the edges pointed in the following image:

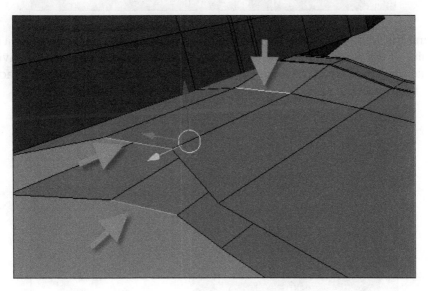

These edges must be scaled up a bit.

As we are looking at the backside of the model, let's close the wings just like we did for the front. Select the edges at the top and bottom of the wing and create a face, as shown in the following image (section A). Just like we did before, add an edge loop to the new face and move it a bit backwards.

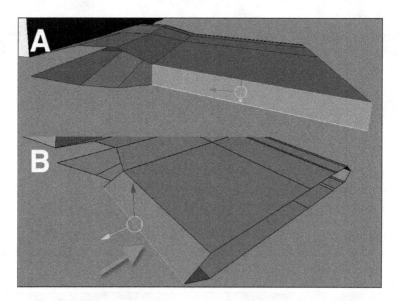

Following the same procedure for the front engine, we will select and create a face at the joint of the wing and engine (section A). The back of the engine will have the same faces and process as the front engine. Select four vertices and create a face (section B). Repeat the same process for the other two faces (section C).

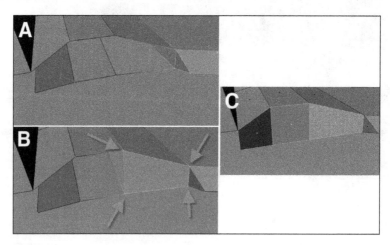

With the faces still selected, we will create a set of extrusions, followed by transformations. The following image shows the creation of three extrusions. For the second and third extrusions, we will move the edges and scale them down.

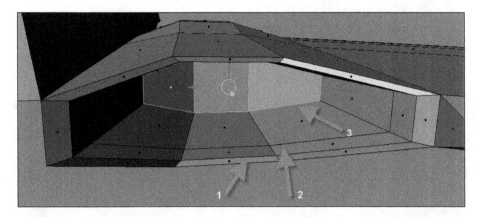

The engine is now created and ready to receive more details and cables, but we must close the remaining parts of the wing before moving further. Select the opposite edges pointed in the following image, and create faces connecting them. Another way to create the faces is by selecting all the edges, creating an extrusion, and snapping the faces.

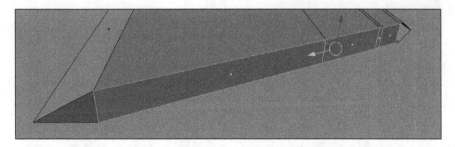

Either way will work, and to finish this part of the wing, we will need an edge loop at the middle of the faces.

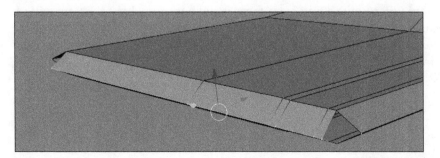

Along with those parts, we have the corners of the wing that are still open. Select the two vertices pointed in the next image (A), and connect them (B):

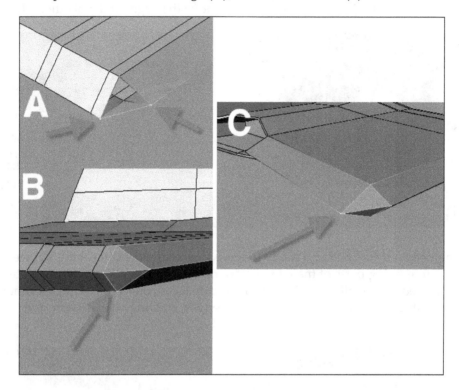

Now, select all the vertices from the corner and press the *F* key to create faces connecting the vertices. Repeat the same procedure for the other corner of the wing (section C).

Creating the bottom of the spacecraft

In the previous sections of the modeling process, we created a lot of small parts and finishing touches for the spacecraft, but we still have more to do. The next part of the model that will receive a few extra faces is the bottom, where the new wing parts will be useful now to help create the bottom faces. Before we do anything, rotate the view to see the bottom part of the spacecraft, and select the edges pointed in the following image:

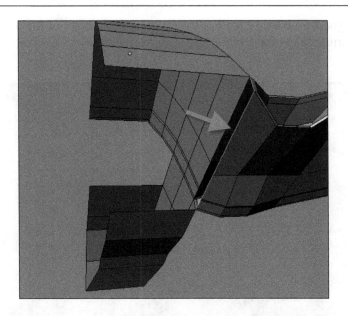

Note that we need only one extrusion to create the new faces and close the bottom. But, to make the placement of the new faces easier, we will use the snap tool of Blender. Before hitting the *E* key, turn on the snap tool.

Create an extrusion and hold down the *Ctrl* key to create the new faces and place them at the right position, shown as a small white circle in the following image:

This will be a good time to align all of the faces at the bottom of the model and all edges. We must select the front edges that were created in the beginning of this chapter.

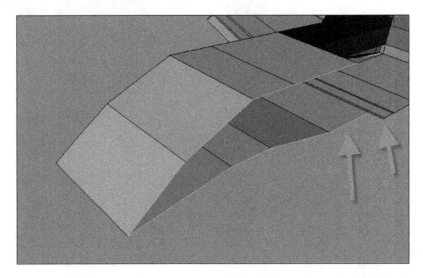

With the snap tool still selected, move the edges until they are aligned to the other edges of the model.

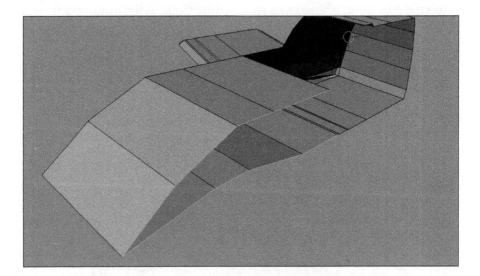

Creating the weapons

Our spacecraft needs a few weapons and guns attached to the wing to make it more interesting. And that's what we will do now! To create guns and weapons for the model, select the faces pointed in the following image and extruding them three times. The object created with this move will be the base for the two weapons that will be attached to the wing.

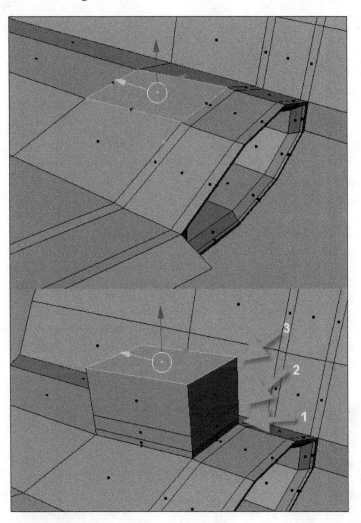

When the extrusions are finished, add two new edge loops to the model right where the next figure shows. Use the middle mouse button to add the loops at the middle point of each face (section A).

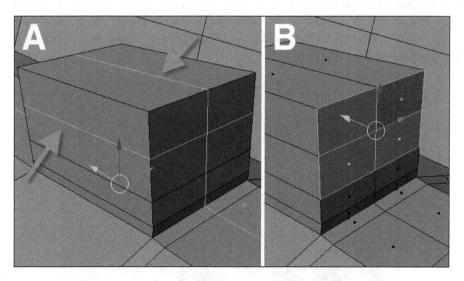

The weapon model that we will create has a cylindrical shape, and to create a shape like this, we need a circle or cylinder to start. There is an easy and quick way to mix the shape of a square and a circle in Blender, which we will see next. To start, select the faces shown in the previous image (section B) and erase them. Erase the faces, but leave the edges around the deleted faces selected.

Set the view to see the model at the front, and with the snap options, align the 3D cursor to the selected edges by pressing *Shift+S* and choosing **Cursor | Selection**. With the cursor aligned, create a mesh circle with eight sides as seen below (section A).

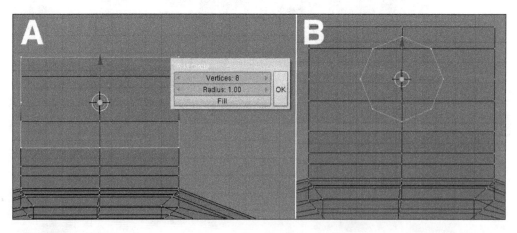

Scale the circle until it looks like the one in the preceding image (section B).

The next step will require a selection made in four vertices that can be converted in a face. Select the vertices and press the *F* key to connect them with a face (section A). Repeat the same process to close all the faces (section B).

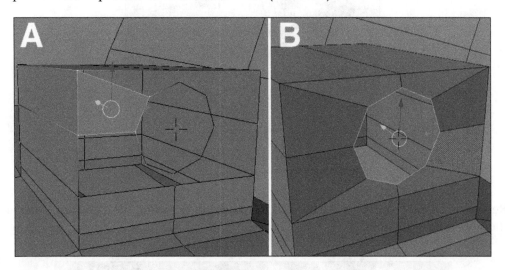

At the end, we will have a circle selected, and it will be the basis to create the weapon. The process will use the same technique that we used to create the engines. With the extrude tool and the scale, apply eleven extrusions and the required transformations to make the gun look like the next image:

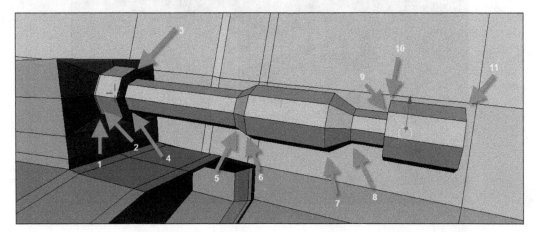

Try to close the front side of the weapon to make it look like the following image:

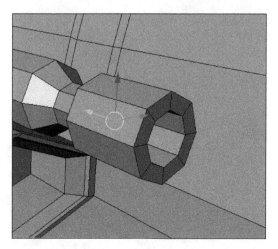

Repeat the same process for the back of the model by selecting the same faces used in the front side of the model.

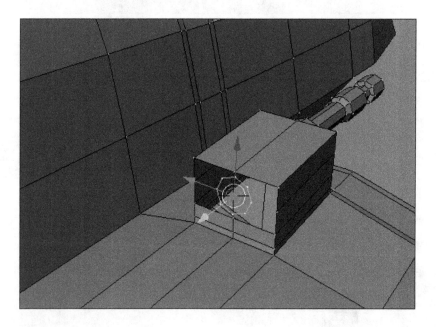

The back of the weapon is simpler than the front and only requires four extrusions.

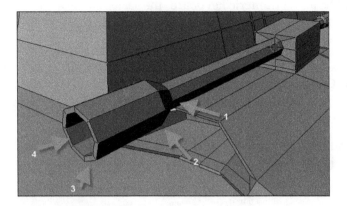

Mirroring the spacecraft

The mirror modifier in Blender is a great tool for symmetrical models like the one we are creating because everything can be created in only one side and copied to the other. Now is a good time to add this modifier and take a look at how our model will be when it's complete. Before the application of an extrusion modifier, we have to make sure that the center point of the object is really at the center.

Change the view to see the model from the top, and select all of the vertices at the right of the model, as shown next (section A). This selection can be made with the border select tool, which is the B key.

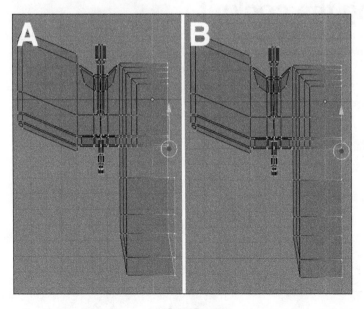

Press the *S* key and the *X* key to constrain the scale to the X axis. Now, if we press the *0* key from the alpha numeric keyboard, the scale will be set to zero and all vertices will be aligned at the same plane (section B).

If the center point of the model is not aligned with those vertices, press the *Shift+S* keys and choose cursor to selection. In the editing panel of Blender, we will find a button called **Center Cursor**, which will set the center point of the object to the position of the 3D cursor. Press this button and the model will be ready to receive a mirror modifier.

This is important to the mirror modifier because it's from the center point that the object will be mirrored. In the modifiers panel, we will find the mirror:

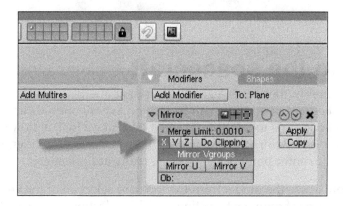

Closing the cockpit

The model is almost ready to receive materials and textures, but there are a few details like the cockpit that requires a few extra details. For instance, we still have to close the cockpit area. In this section of the project, we will use a trick to create a new shape based on a selection. This will allow us to use a shape to create another, making the process a lot easier.

The first step is to select the edge pointed in the following image:

Turn the snap tool on and extrude the edge until it closes the upper part of the cockpit. Now, select the three edges pointed in the left image (section A). The trick now will be to duplicate the edges with the *Shift+D* keys and then cancel the placement of the copies by using the *Esc* key. The copies will still be selected, and with them selected, we will press the *P* key (section B). This key will separate the objects into two, and for us, the selected option will be enough to create a new object based on the selected edges.

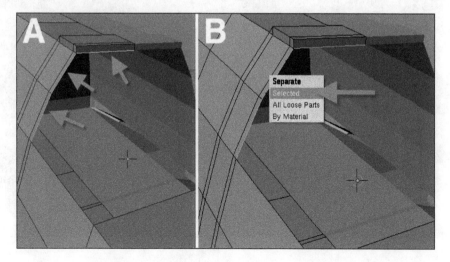

Go to object mode, and select the new object created based on the edges. Enter in edit mode, and extrude the edges, as shown in the following screenshot:

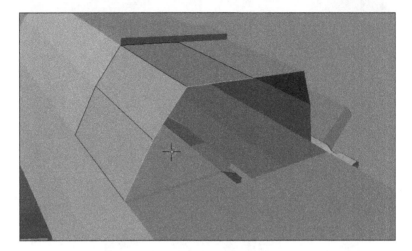

To close down the cockpit, we will need to use a spin tool. Before we use the spin tool, we have to follow two simple steps:

1. Set the center point of the spin.
2. Change the view to make it perpendicular to the spin.

Now, select the vertex pointed out in the next screenshot, and snap the 3D cursor to it. The 3D cursor will mark the center of the spin.

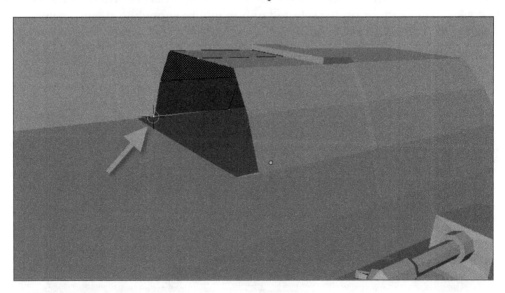

Change the view to the model on the side, and set up the spin. For this model, the settings were changed to have 4 steps, and the rotation was set as clockwise.

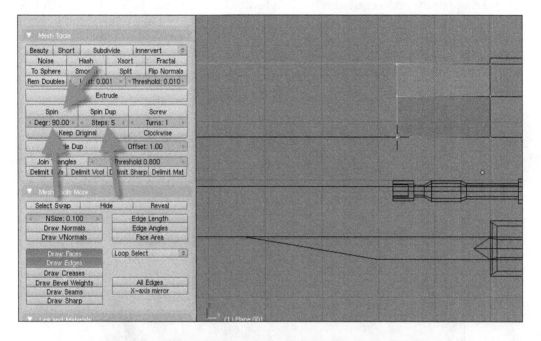

After pressing the **Spin** button, we will see the cockpit closed.

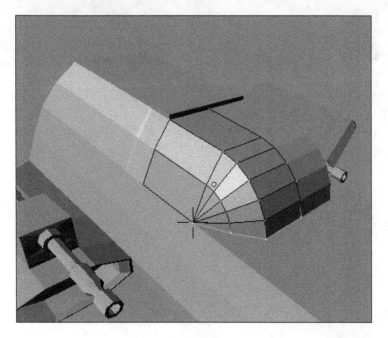

Detailing the fuselage

The fuselage of the spacecraft also needs a few details to make the machine complete, and by the reference image presented in the last chapter, we have a few details attached to the fuselage. For details like the ones we will be creating, the trick used to create objects based on the shape of another will be very useful because those details follow the same shape of the main object.

To start, we will add an edge loop to the back of the spacecraft.

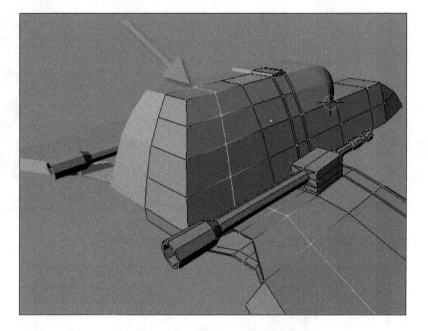

When the edge loop is created, select only the faces pointed in the following image (section A). With the faces selected, press the *Shift+D* keys to duplicate the faces and move them just a bit to the right. Press the *E* key to extrude the faces and create a small volume at the side of the model (section B).

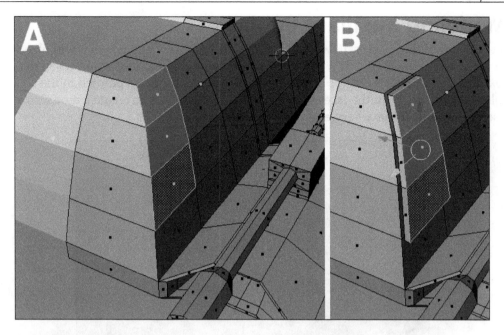

To finish this detail, we must select the middle back face and extrude it just a bit.

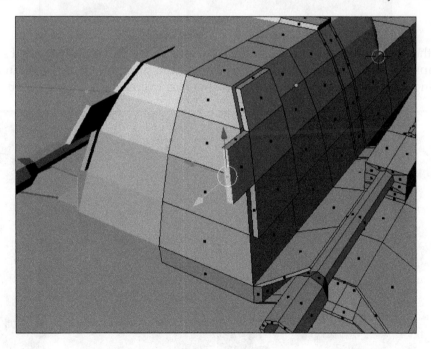

Modeling auxiliary engines

At the back of the spacecraft, we will create some auxiliary engines that will blend in the shape of the model. It will look like something made out of wood when the textures and materials are applied to the model. Select the faces pointed in the following image. With the faces selected, extrude them back to create a new shape used to support the auxiliary engines.

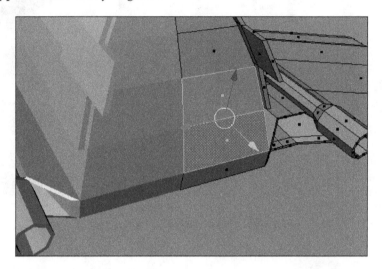

When the extrusion is created, select the face right above the recently created shape and duplicate it. Move it away from the original face, and place it as shown in the following image (section A). Now, extrude the face to create a solid (section B).

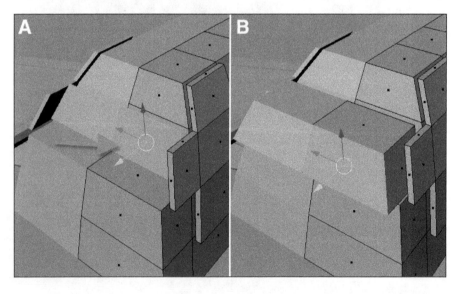

With a sequence of extrudes and scale transformations, create a hole in the solid like the one in the following image:

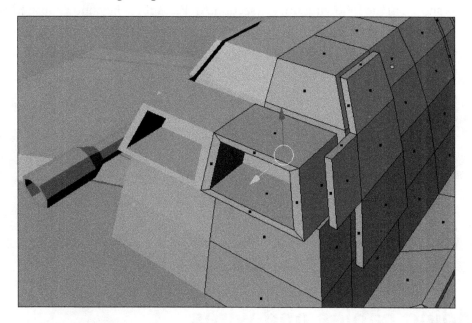

We have to create a connection between the new engines and the main body of the spacecraft. Let's create something like a wooden arm holding the engine. Select the top face, and with the extrusion and scale transformation, create a shape like the one in the following image (section A). Repeat the same process for the face above the main body. To finish the process, select each of the small faces created, and extrude them two times (section B). We will have the basis of both arms created.

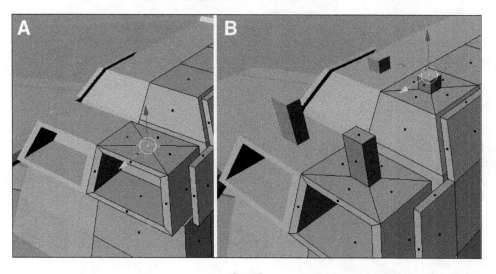

At the top of each arm, we have to create a small extrusion to make two parallel faces. Those faces will be the basis for the connection between both arms. Select both faces as shown in the following image (section A). Press the *F* key and choose **Skin Faces/Edge-Loops** (section B).

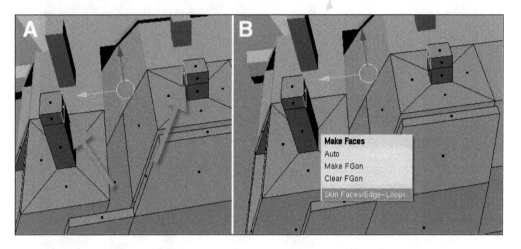

Adding cables and wires

A spacecraft without some cables and wires would look weird; even a steampunk machine needs some cables and wires to look like a real machine. But, as we are dealing with a sci-fi vehicle, there is nothing wrong with placing those cables and wires outside of the wing shell. The best way to create cables and wires in Blender is by using a combination of curves and surfaces with a tool called **BevOb**. With this option, we can draw a curve and determine the shape of the wire with a surface.

It works just like an extrusion along a path, with the option to later convert this geometry to mesh and apply the same modifiers and tools that we are used to work with shapes like planes and primitive meshes.

Using curves

To use curves, we have to add a new type of object that hasn't been used in this book so far—the curve object. The process of manipulating a curve is different from a mesh object, and that's why we need to keep a few things in mind. There are three types of curves in Blender, all of them with specific controls and effects on the shape of the curve:

- **Automatic**: With this type of curve, we can move each control point independently, but their rotation will affect the control point on the opposite side.

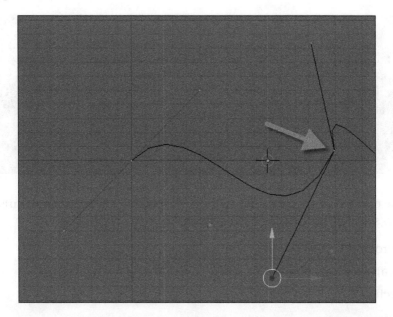

- **Free/Aligned**: Here, we have a type of control point that can be totally independent of the movement and rotation (**Free**) and another one that will make the rotation of the control points affect the opposite control (**Aligned**).

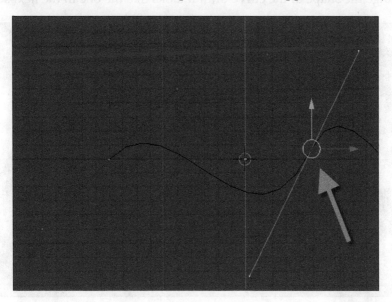

- **Vector**: The control points here are completely independent like the **Free** curve, but the difference is that there won't be any curves around a control point here. The lines around a point will form a corner instead of a curve.

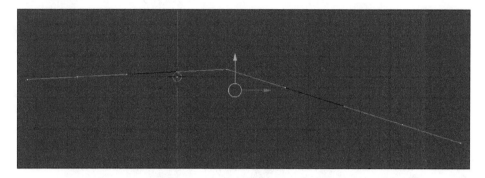

All of these curve types can be used with the respective keyboard short cuts when the curve is selected and we are in edit mode:

- Automatic: *Shift+H*
- Swap Free and Aligned: *H*
- Vector: *V*

For our cables and wires, we will be using the Aligned type, but you are free to make changes and adjustments and try a different type of curve. The first thing to do is to add a new curve to the scene, and immediately (while we are still in edit mode) change the shape of the curve until it looks like the one in the next screenshot:

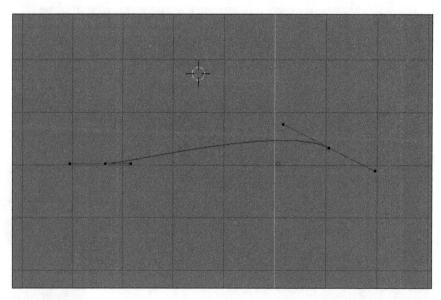

The curve is the path where we will place our cables and wires, which will really be created with a profile. For this profile, add another curve and, this time, choose a curve circle object. Now, without leaving the edit mode, make some duplicates of these circles until you get a shape like the one shown next. A curve is defined by two points that connect with a line, which is actually the curve. The control handles are located at the extremity of each curve and can deform the orientation of the line.

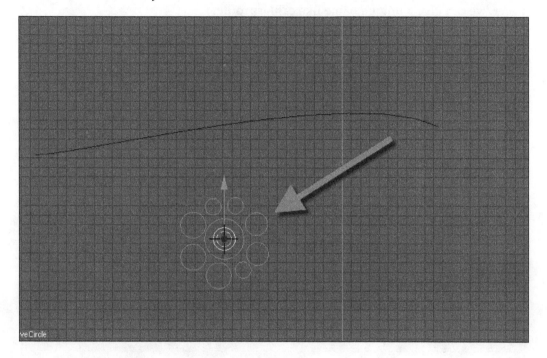

ve Circle

Now, with the object name in mind, we can select the curve that will work as a path again. Go to the **Edit** panel and locate the **BevOb** option, which is located right below the menu. In the **BevOb** text area, enter the name of the curve, and the result will be a shape similar to some cables placed along a long path. If you don't know the name of the curve, just select the object and press the *N* key. A small menu will appear, and in the OB field, we will see the name of the object. To make this process easier, we can give a unique name like **cablesprofile**.

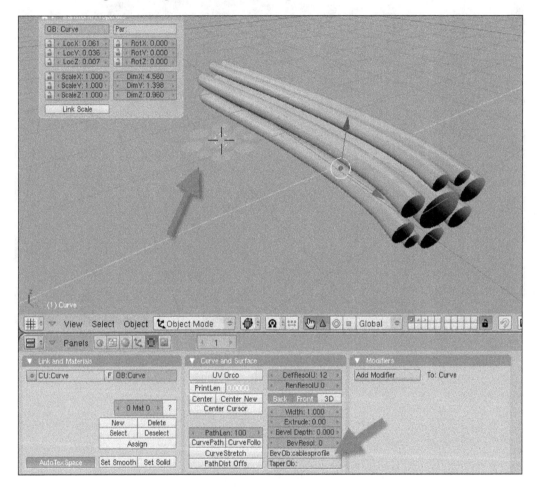

Use this same technique to create new cables and wires along the sides of the wing and main structure of the spacecraft. Now all we have to do is select the control points and edit the position. If the curve needs more control points, select one point at the beginning or end of the curve, and while holding down the *Ctrl* key, right-click anywhere to add a new point.

Twisting the cables

The placement of some cables is not enough to give an impression of realism to those objects, and we could use some extra tools to give the object a twist. Actually, the twist will bend the cables along their axis and give the impression of a real installation of wires in the wing area. To do that, we will use a tool called **Tilt**, which can rotate the normals of a curve. This tool works with the *T* key short cut and has to be used in the edit mode of a curve while some points are selected. Before pressing the *T* key, make sure that you turn on the 3D button in the curve and surface menu, because only 3D curves can be modified by the tilt option.

Here is an example of what we can do with the tilt tool. Selecting one of our cables and applying a tilt will result in a structure like this:

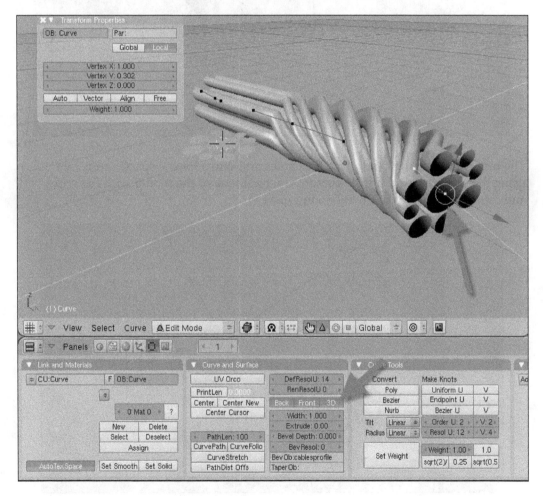

The twisting of those cables can be made manually as well.

Adding the cables to the model

Now that we know how to add cables and wires to the scene, we can work on the model to create a few of those details. This is what the spacecraft looks like now:

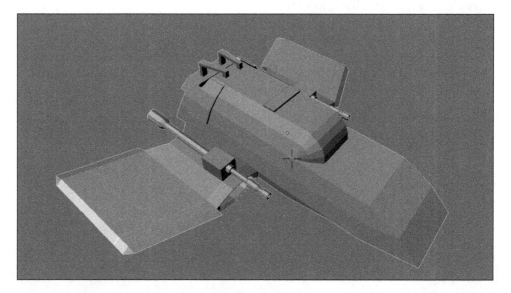

The best way to control and place the cables and wires for the spacecraft is by using the snap tool and the 3D cursor. The final look of the model with the wires and cables can be seen in the following image:

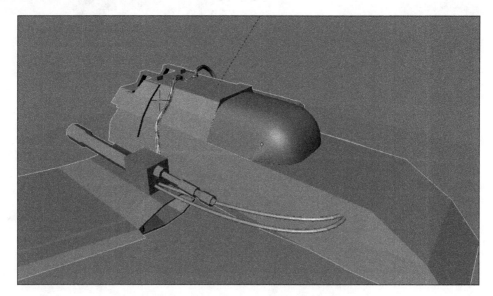

Place the 3D cursor at the center of the face shown in the following image and create a curve. Select the end of this curve and, using the snap tool, place the control point of the curve aligned to the 3D cursor.

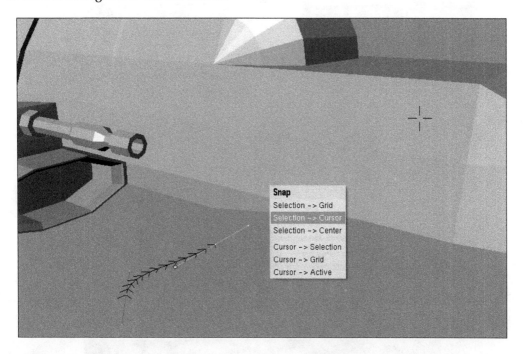

Repeat the same process for the other extremity of the curve.

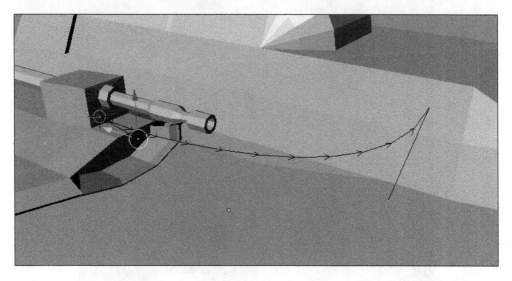

Add another curve and change the alignment to make it look like the first curve, with only a small difference in the placement.

To finish with the curves, add another one aligned to the top of the spacecraft and connected with the wing.

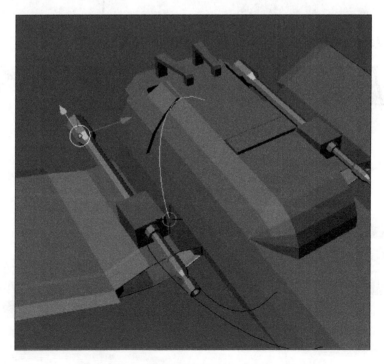

Summary

In this chapter, we added more details to our spacecraft and, in the process, learned some new techniques to use with Blender.

Here is a quick summary of what we have learned:

- How to use the spin tool to create rounded bevels
- How to create shapes from existing geometry
- How to apply edge modeling to create geometry
- How to work with the different curves of Blender
- How to create cables and wires with curves
- How to twist curves

8
Advanced UV Mapping

In this chapter, we will learn how to add a few extra details with textures, which can be a great help in any modeling project. For our spacecraft, the textures will add objects and textures that could make the overall model hard to finish. One advantage of using a great set of textures to create details is the ability to use images instead of models to create geometry. This is possible because textures create shadows and the impression of depth in models.

UV mapping in Blender

The textures in Blender are divided into two main types: **procedural textures** and **image-based textures**. With procedural textures, the organization and distribution of textures along the 3D object is rather simple, and all we have to do is choose the type of mapping that fits the shape of the object such as a cube, cylinder, and so on. However, with image-based textures, it's harder to control exactly where each part of the image texture will be placed.

If we have an image texture to place in a 3D model, we can distribute the image with a tiling layout. For simple and quick scenes, the tiling layout may work well, but when it's necessary to have full control over textures, it's unenviable to turn into UV Mapping.

What is UV mapping?

UV mapping is a way to apply a texture to an object with full control of each part of the texture. When working with UV textures, we have to follow three basic steps before applying any type of texture:

1. Mark the model with seams to unfold it into a 2D set of planes.
2. Export the unfolded mesh to a texture map.
3. Paint the textures over the texture map.

Only when we have the painted texture map will we be able to apply the textures with full control over the object.

The downside of UV mapping is that it's geometry dependent, and every time a change is applied to the 3D model that alters the topology or poly count, the mapping and organization of the model must be created all over again. To avoid those types of problems, begin working with UVs only when the model is complete and no changes are planned.

Another downside is the process of marking the model with seams, which can be difficult at first glance. The hard part of marking seams in edges of the model is that we have to find key loops in the model to better unfold it down. All solutions we find to unfold a model only apply to the specific model that we are working on and cannot be used in other projects.

In Blender, we have a few scripts that do the unfolding of the 3D model automatically. This can be a time-saver when we can't find the best way to mark the seams. A good reason to pick UV mapping to texture our project is that YafaRay, and almost all other external renderers that support Blender, can only display textures in 3D models if we use UV mapping. All models exported to these renderers with textures applied without UVs won't appear at the rendering.

For our project, we will use YafaRay as renderer, which is another reason to use UV mapping to set up our textures.

Using UV mapping in Blender

Before we begin working on the spacecraft model, let's learn how UV mapping works in Blender. To use UV mapping in Blender 3D, we can go by two different ways, which will allow us to work faster, but with less control over the organization of unwrapping. Or, we can have full control of the process, but there will be some extra work in the setup. Both methods work just fine for any type of project, and we will take a look at how each of them works. The first method involves the use of a powerful script from Blender called **Unwrap (smart projections)**. This script was developed to automatically find the best way to unwrap the mesh of any selected 3D model and allow an artist to quickly create UV textures. The downside is that we will lose control of the faces' placement in the texture map.

However, for some artists, the loss of control over where each part of the model will be organized can't be compared with the gain in speed. With only a few mouse clicks, we can have a fully unwrapped 3D model. The difference between the traditional hand edition of the unwrapping process and the use of a script is only at the beginning of the process; by the time a model is unwrapped, we will export a bitmap image to be edited in GIMP or Photoshop.

The other method involves the hand edition of a 3D model to unwrap it manually. This is done by the addition of a seam to the 3D model, which is used by the unwrap tool to split and unfold the model. This method allows full control over the process, but may seem a bit challenging for some artists, because it will force them to plan how the model will be unfolded. For our spacecraft model, we can use any method, and to better illustrate when we can use each technique, we will take a closer look at how to work with each method in the next section.

Using smart projections

Smart projections is the tool that allows us to create fast UV layouts and unfold a mesh with only a few mouse clicks. To use the tool, select a 3D mesh model and change the work mode to the edit mode. All operations that use UV mapping of a 3D model are created in a window called **UV/Image Editor**. Create a new window in the Blender 3D interface, and change the window type to UV/Image Editor.

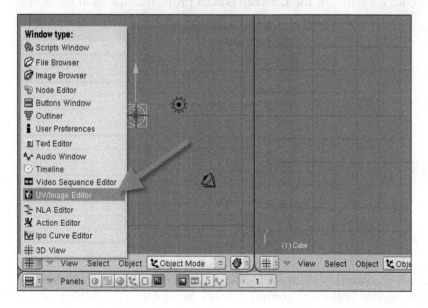

After opening the **UV/Image Editor** window and setting the work mode to edit, select all objects of the 3D model, such as vertices, edges, or faces, and press the *U* key. It will open the **Unwrap** menu with several options.

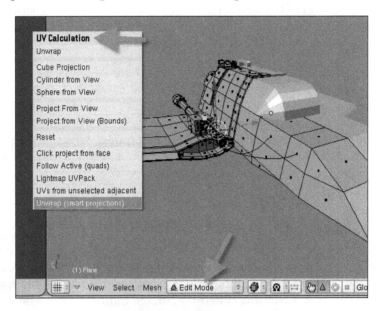

In this menu, we will find the **Unwrap (smart projections)** tool at the bottom.

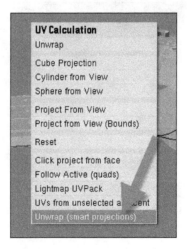

If we choose the smart projections tool, a new menu will appear. In this menu, we can choose several options to control the way in which all projections are created. It's not as flexible as working with seams, but with this option, a few aspects of the tool can be controlled.

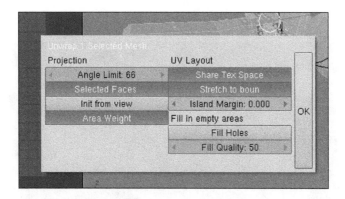

The menu is divided in two sections, controlling the projection of the 3D model on the left and the UV layout on the right. From the projection controls, one of the most important parameters is the angle value. Every time we use smart projections, the result will be a set of faces organized as a flat object. As there are a lot of ways to organize the faces of a 3D model over a flat surface, we must have a way to control how distorted they will be, or how many groups will be created from each section of the 3D model. The angle parameter controls exactly this type of layout.

For instance, let's apply the smart projections to the wing of the spacecraft with different values for the angle. First, we have to select only the faces of the wing, and in the edit mode, press the *U* key. For this first example, we will use the default value of 66 for the angle.

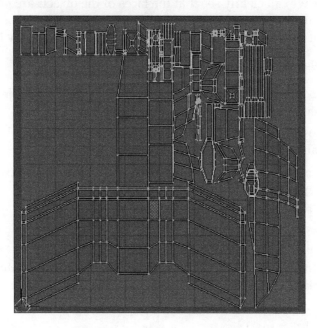

Now, let's create another UV layout with the angle set to 89.

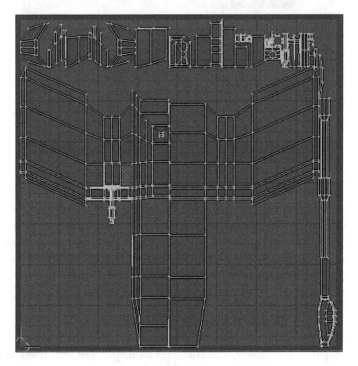

In the last image, we can clearly see that the faces of the objects are grouped in fewer islands, while in the image representing the smart projections with a default angle of 66, the number of faces spread around the UV layout is significantly higher.

The other controls for smart projections are as follows:

- **Share Tex Space**: By using this option, we will make the objects share the space used by the texture of the UV layout.

- **Stretch to bound**: If this button is clicked, the unwrapped objects will stretch to the bounds of the UV layout.

- **Island Margin**: Here, we can add a margin to the face groups to avoid overlapping.

- **Fill Holes**: By using this button, we will force the filling of empty areas in the UV layout. Use this control with caution because the calculations may take a while depending on the complexity of the 3D model.

- **Fill Quality**: Here, we can set the quality of the fill used in the **Fill Holes** option.

UV test grid

How will we know if the unwrapped faces aren't stretched or deformed by the process? To determine this, we use something called a test grid. It's an automated image that can be created by Blender in the **UV/Image Editor** window to show us how the texture is distributed over the object's surface.

To create a test grid, just press the *Alt+N* keys in the UV/Image Editor when a model is unwrapped. This short cut creates a new image based on some information provided in a small menu. In this menu, we can set the image to be a UV test grid by pressing the **UV Test Grid** button. In addition, increase the size of the image in order to produce a high quality image. For this example, the images were set to **Width** of **2056** pixels and a **Height** of **2056** pixels.

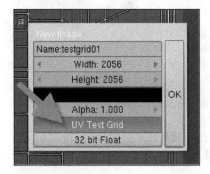

The test grid will look like an image full of small squares painted gray with small marks at the center of each square. Notice that these squares and the colors in their centers are only indented to help the visualization of the UV layout. Now, we can change the **Draw** mode in the 3D view to texture, and we will see the 3D model textured with the test grid. With this test grid, we can compare the way an image is textured with the signs in the grid.

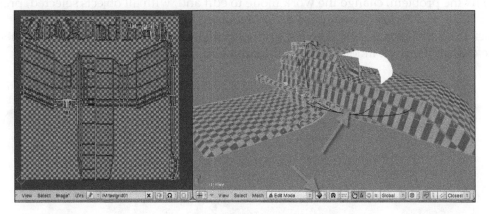

Notice that by using a test grid, we can identify problems like stretched faces. The following image shows a few faces on the side of the spacecraft with stretched UVs:

We should have squares from the test grid, but instead, we see rectangles. This is clearly a problem that will be reflected during rendering. To fix this problem, we have two options:

- Use the smart projections again, but with a lower angle in the layout options
- Edit the UV layout manually

For now, we will change the angle of the smart projections. Later in this chapter, we will learn how to manually control the UVs.

To fix the problem, change the work mode to edit and, with all objects selected, press the *U* key and choose **Unwrap (smart projections)** again. Change the angle value back to 66 and click on **OK**. The test grid will still be applied to the model and when we change the work mode to object, the stretching problem will be fixed.

To erase the test grid, just go to the **UV/Image Editor** window with the 3D model selected. In edit mode, press the **X** button at the right of the image map name.

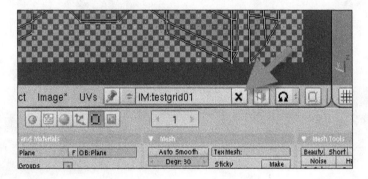

Removing a texture

When we remove a texture like the test grid while in **Textured** draw mode, the object will look all white. Change the draw mode to wireframe or shaded to correct the visualization.

Using the unwrap tool

With smart projections, we have a quick way to work with UV textures. This tool allows us to do all the processing with only a few mouse clicks. If we want to take full control over the process, however, we will have to use special controls to change the UV mapping layout. To unwrap using those tools, we have to plan the unwrap creation before anything else.

Planning the unwrap

For a good unwrap, we must first create groups of vertices that will be unfolded together in the process. As the unwrapping will end up with a flat model, we can split the spacecraft in small parts, which will be marked by seams. These seams work like a knife that cuts the model and creates a flat model separated by marks. Keep the following two tips in mind when cutting the model with seams:

- Group the faces in similar textures
- Make the unwrapped surface easy to edit in GIMP or Photoshop by identifying each part

A great way to start is by creating a test cut by adding a new UV layout. In Blender, we can add as many layouts as we need by using the button pointed in the following image:

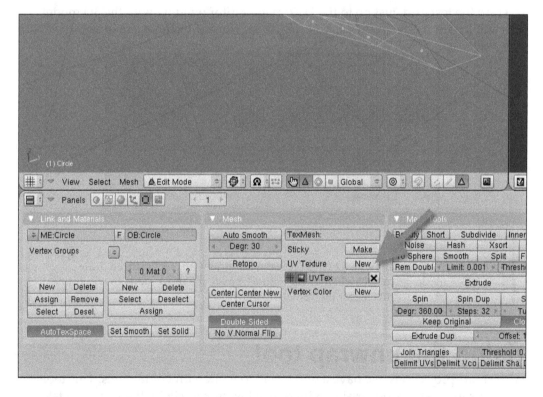

If we press the button labeled **New**, a new UV layout will be created in Blender, and we will be able to select this new layout by using the selector at the bottom of the UV/Image Editor window. We can create as many UV layouts as we want. These UV layouts will be displayed on the UV/Image Editor window. No matter how many of them we have, only one can be displayed in the UV/Image Editor and one can be used for rendering. We will make our choice using the small icons on the left of the UV names. The icon with a small grid will set the active UV layout and the other with a portrait will make the UV to be used for rendering.

This is a tool used to add several layers of UVs staked on each other to blend textures and create advanced effects. For instance, we can add a clean texture at one UV and then add another one to paint and make the texture look old. Add a texture layout is the same as opening the UV/Image Editor window. With an object selected, press the *U* key. A new UV layout will be created.

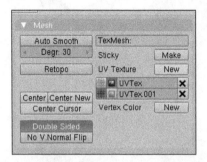

With a new UV created, we can go to the **Edge Specials** menu where we will find the Mark Seam option to pick the edges that will be used to cut the 3D model. In the edit mode, press the *Ctrl+E* keys to open the specials menu.

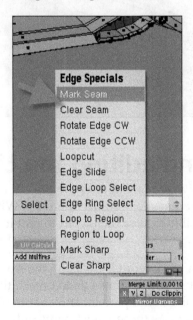

At the top of the menu, we will find the **Mark Seam** and **Clear Seam** options, which are used to mark or unmark an edge to be used in the unwrapping process. When an edge is marked with a seam, it will be separated into two edges during the unwrapping process. If we choose all edges of a model and mark them with a seam, the result will be a lot of small faces spread around the UV layout. That's the reason we choose only a few key edges to mark as a seam.

When an edge is marked as a seam, its color will change to orange.

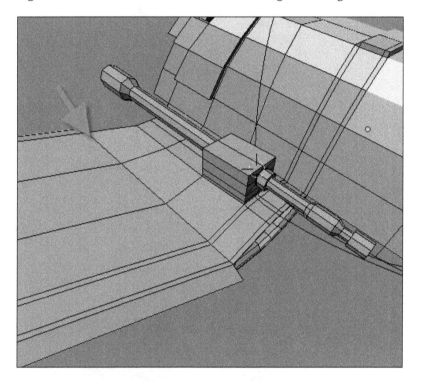

Controlling and editing the UV layout

Now that we already know a bit more about how the UV tools of Blender 3D work, we will use some interactive tools to organize the UV's. When the unfolded mesh is organized, it will be possible to save the layout to edit it in any image editor like GIMP or Photoshop.

The fastest way to create an UV Layout is by using the smart projections option we saw earlier in this chapter, which allows us to unfold the mesh with only a few mouse clicks. It's a great tool, but not perfect, and eventually it will need a few adjustments to work properly. As those adjustments only involve small parts of the model, we can block the editing of the parts with the correct UV Layout.

Pinning and unpinning vertices

We can do this with a tool called **Pin**, which blocks the transformation of a vertex from an unfolded mesh. If we have to apply the Unwrap tool again, the layout of the pinned vertices will be saved. To add a pin to a vertex, select one or more vertices and press the *P* key, or use the UV menu and choose **Pin**. The vertex will be marked with a red dot showing that it has a pin.

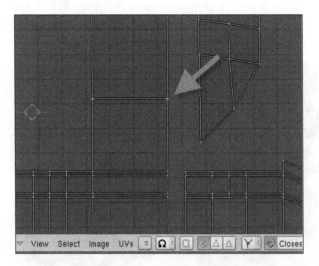

To unpin a vertex, select the vertices and press *Alt+P*, or choose **Unpin** from the UV menu.

Live Unwrap Transform

One of the most powerful tools to Unwrap models in Blender 3D is the **Live Unwrap Transform** tool, which can transform and adapt the unfolded mesh in real time. To use this feature, we have to turn the **Live Unwrap** in the UV menu on.

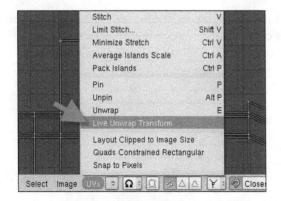

To see **Live Unwrap Transform** in action, we have to select a pinned vertex and move it around. This will trigger the **Live Unwrap** option, and we will see the unfolded mesh adapts and change in real time.

Editing the UV

We have seen all the tools and options needed to edit the UV mapping of the spacecraft. Now, we can define the final layout of the model. Unfold the mesh and make the UV look like the layout shown in the following image:

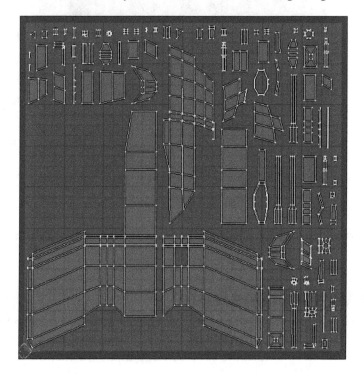

The faces are spread along the layout, but it will allow individual control over the texture for each face of the model. To connect the faces to each other, we can use the snap tools available in the UV/Image Editor window; they work exactly in the same way like the 3D view. There we will find:

- 3D Cursor
- Snap tools (*Shift+S* keys)
- Vertex snap

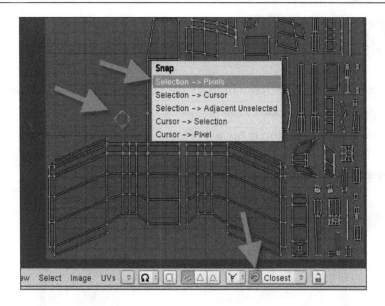

Exporting the layout

The last step in sending the UV Layout to an external image editor is to save the layout as a bitmap image, with the script called **Save UV Face Layout...** in the UV menu. This script will generate a TGA file with the layout ready to be edited.

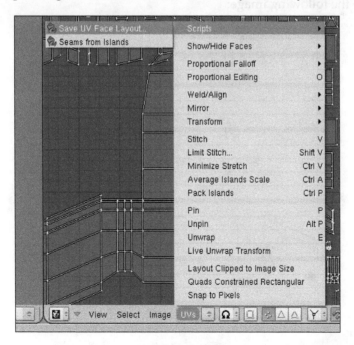

These are the options that will appear when setting up the layout:

- **Size**: Size in pixels of the UV Layout. Choose a high size to work with details in the texture
- **Wire**: Size of the line that will mark the edges of the unfolded mesh
- **Wrap**: Change the scale of the layout
- **All Faces**: If this button is turned off, only the selected faces will be exported
- **Object**: Uses the object name in the TGA filename

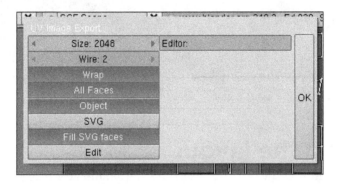

For this model, we will use a **Size** of **2048** and a **Wire** of **2**. The layout will be exported like the following image:

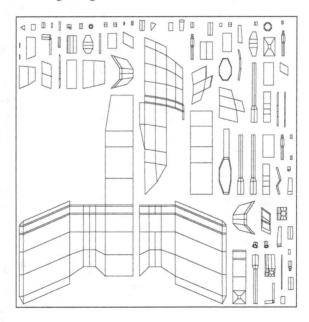

Editing the texture

In the last section, we saw how to export the UV Layout as a bitmap file, ready to be edited in software such as GIMP or Photoshop. Now, we have to open one of those software and start painting the textures, logos, characters, and other elements that will compose the texture of the spacecraft. For our spacecraft, the texture used will be an old metallic plate, pasted over the faces as shown in the following screenshot:

When the texture is edited and saved as a PNG or JPG file (PNG is preferred in order to maintain the quality), we can apply the texture to the spacecraft in Blender 3D. To do that, we have to assign the texture to the material applied to the model.

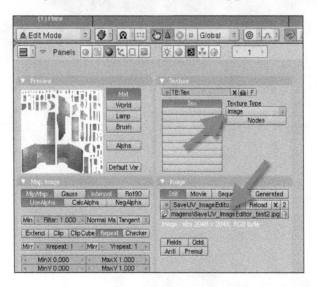

From the **Map Input** menu press the **UV** button.

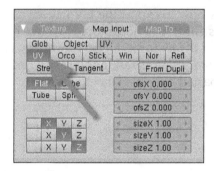

To verify that everything is placed correctly, we can open the image in the UV/Image editor and choose **Textured** as the draw type to be displayed in the 3D view.

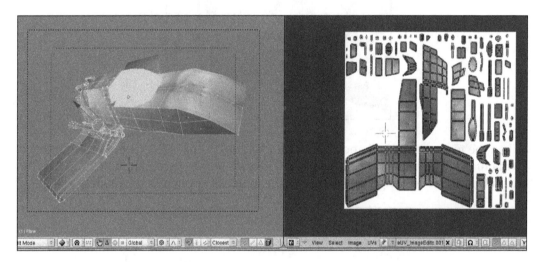

If the texture shows at the 3D view, it will appear when we render the project with YafaRay.

Summary

In this chapter, we learned how to use some of the advanced texturing options of Blender, change the way a texture is placed along with the object, and even painted the image only using Blender.

Here is a list of things that we have learned in this chapter:

- How to control the UV mapping in Blender
- How to create a test grid
- How to add layered UV layouts
- How to use the snapping tools to organize the unfolded mesh
- How to edit and change the UV layout
- How to export the UV layout to image editors
- How to edit a texture
- How to apply the texture back to an object

9
Putting the Spacecraft to Fly and Shoot with Special Effects

In this chapter, we will use special effects to put our spacecraft in outer space and even make both weapons shoot! These effects will be created with a mix of particles and composition nodes that will generate the effects in a very short time. Both techniques and tools will help a lot in this project, and both can be used in other 3D modeling and rendering projects as well.

Blender particles

In the last versions of Blender 3D, the particle system received a huge upgrade, making it more complex and powerful than before. This upgrade, however, made it necessary to create more parameters and options in order for the system to acts. What didn't change was the need for an object that works as emitter of the particles. The shape and look of this object will be directly related to the type of effects we want to create.

Before we discuss the effects that we will be creating, let's look at how the particles work in Blender. To create any type of particle system, go to the **Objects** panel and find the **Particles** button.

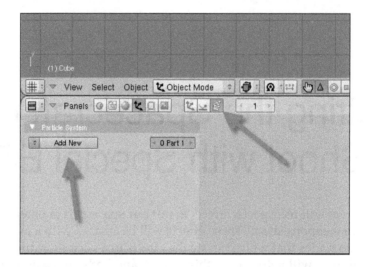

This is where we will set up and change our particles for a variety of effects. The first time we open this menu, nothing will be displayed. But, if we select a mesh object and press the **Add New** button, this object will immediately turn into a new emitter.

When a new emitter is created, we have to choose the type of behavior this emitter has in the particle system. In the top-left part of the menu, we will find a selector that lets us choose the type of interaction of the emitter.

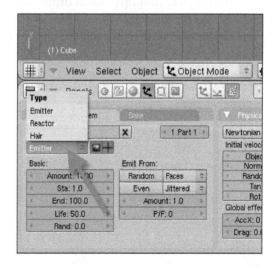

These are the three types of emitters:

1. **Emitter**: This is the standard type, which is a single object that emits particles according to the parameters and rules that we set up in the particles controls.

2. **Hair**: Here, we have a type of particle emitter that creates particles as thin lines for representing hair and fur. Since this is more related to characters, we won't use this type of emitter in this book.

3. **Reactor**: With this emitter, we can create particle systems that interact with each other. It works by setting up a particle system that interferes with the motion and changes the trajectories of other particles.

In our projects, we will use only the emitter type. However, you can create indirect animations and use particles to interact with each other. For instance, if you want to create a set of asteroids that block the path of our spacecraft, we could create this type of animation easily with a reactor particle system.

How particles work

To create and use a particle system, we will look at the most important features and parameters of each menu and create some pre-systems to use later in this chapter for the spacecraft. To fully understand how particles work, we have to become familiar with the forces or parameters that control the look and feel of particles. For each of those parameters and forces, we have a corresponding menu in Blender.

Here corresponding parameters that control the particle system:

- **Quantity**: This is a basic feature of any particle system that allows us to set up how many particles will be in the system.

- **Life**: As a particle system is based on animation parameters, we have to know from how many frames the particle will be visible in the 3D world.

- **Mesh emitting**: Our emitters are all meshes, and we have to determine from which part of those 3D objects the particles will be emitted. We have several options to choose from, such as vertices or parts of the objects delimited by vertex groups.

- **Motion**: If we set up our particle system and don't give it enough force to make the particles move, nothing will happen to the system. So, even more important than setting up the appearance of the particles is choosing the right forces for the initial velocity of the particles.

- **Physics and forces**: Along with the forces that we use in the motion option, we will also apply some force fields and deflectors to particles to simulate and change the trajectories of the objects based on physical reactions.

- **Visualization**: A standard particle system has only small dots as particles, but we can change the way particles look in a variety of ways. To create flares and special effects such as the ones we need, we can use mesh objects that have Halo effects and many more.

- **Interaction**: At the end of the particle life, we can use several types of actions and behaviors to control the destiny of a particle. Should it spawn a new particle or simply die when it hits a special object?

These are the things we have to consider before we begin setting up the animation.

Creating particles

With the rules and the overall setup of the particles in mind, we can move on to the actual setup of the particles. First, let's create a mesh object to use as an emitter, and for that we will create a mesh circle. In order to set up the circle, choose eight vertices and press the **Fill** button. Right after the circle is created, subdivide the object three times until we get an object like the one shown in the following image. As particles are emitted by vertices or faces, it's quite important to have an object with plenty of both.

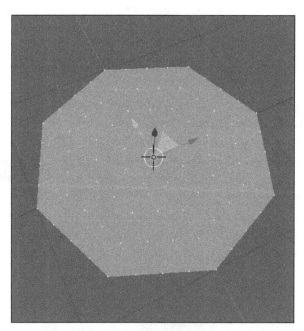

When the circle is finally created, just open the object panel and choose the particle buttons option. Click on the **Add New** button to create a new particle system, and we will be ready to start. Don't worry if nothing seems to happen when the particle system is created; it's because none of the required elements that make a particle system are set yet. The first thing to do when the particle system is created is to add more particles to the animation. In the **Amount** option set the total number to 20000.

In the other parameters of the basic elements, choose the following settings:

- **Sta: 10.0**
- **End: 90.0**
- **Life: 80.0**
- **Rand: 1.0**

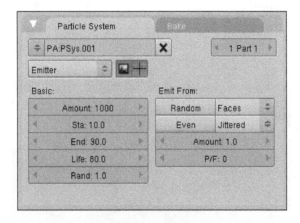

These parameters will generate a particle system like the one shown in the following screenshot:

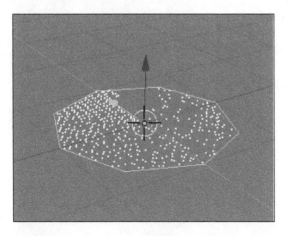

If you can't see any difference in the particles, just move the playback head that controls animation in Blender, and you will see the particles showing up. We can control the animation by using the directional arrows from the keyboard, or we can open a timeline window to see the playback head.

The timeframe between the death and birth of the particles will define how far they will go from the emitter. Together with the life value, it will give the size of the trail of the particles. For us, this set of parameters is very important because we will use them to create the explosive forces going out of the engines. The last parameter randomizes start, end, and life of the particles by a percentage. The number 1 means we are using fifty percent of the random values to generate the particles.

Note the way all particles are being emitted from the faces or vertices. The best way to set up the particles for our project is by using faces only. Set it to emit randomly from the faces by pressing the random button right next to the basic options.

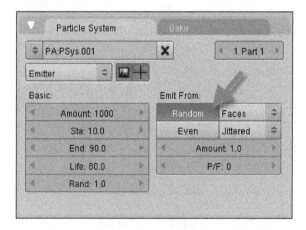

Adding speed and force fields

The particle system is already created, but it's moving at a regular speed and with no influence from force fields around it. To create and add those forces, we will go to the **Physics** menu of the particles, and there we will find the options to change the force and the speed of the particle system. For instance, if we want to add an extra force to the particle motion based on the direction of the normals of each face, just increase the value of the parameter Normal in the Physics menu.

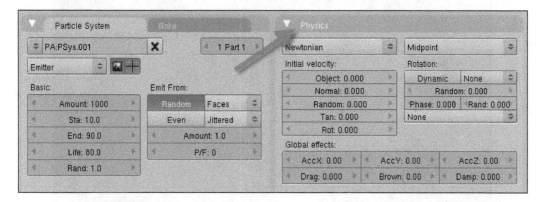

There are other types of forces that we can use to add speed, like the object itself or the surface tangents.

But, what if the particles come under the force of an explosion or other effect that makes them change the original trajectory? In this case, we can use the options located at the bottom of the menu — **AccX**, **AccY**, and **AccZ**. Each of these options can add a force in the respective axis that will influence the direction and speed of the particle system.

Here is an example of a particle system with a force set to **3** in the Y axis:

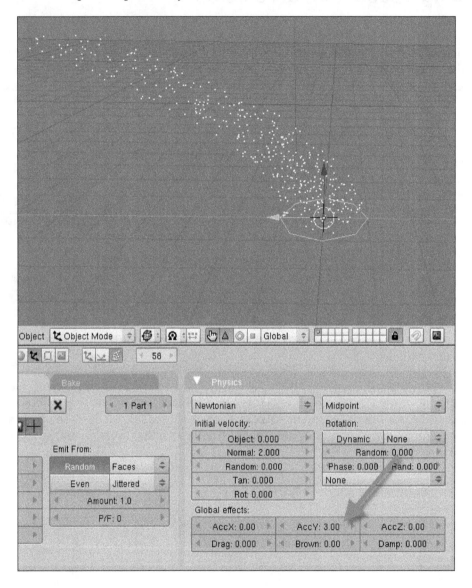

Fortunately, we have a set of options to set up the angle and rotation of the particles as they go out of the emitter. We will use the rotation option in the **Physics** menu to change the rotation of the particles and make them go through a wider angle.

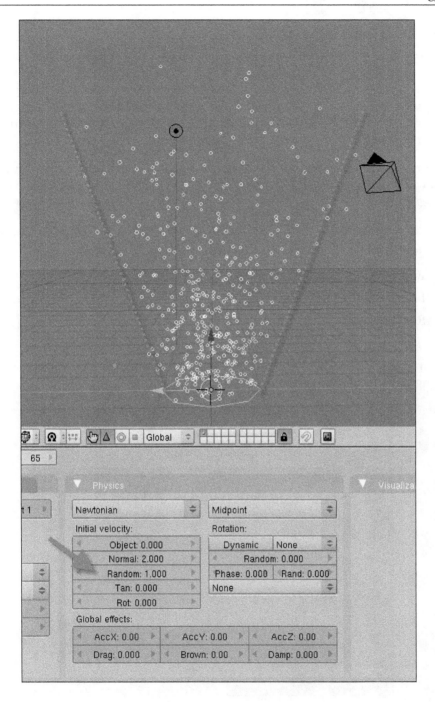

The rear engine

Now that we know a bit more about the particles and how to control them, we can add some objects and particle systems to the rear engine. The purpose of these particle systems is to create an effect of a combustion engine, dumping energy into outer space. To do that, we will use a mix of particles and nodes to create a glow effect. First, add a circle with the approximate same size of the opening for the engine at the back.

Make sure that the circle has several subdivisions on its faces; otherwise, our particle system won't work very well. When the circle is set and created, set up the particles with these settings:

- **Amount: 3000.0**
- **Sta: 10.0**
- **End: 90.0**
- **Life: 80.0**
- **Rand: 2.0**

Change the initial velocity of the particles to **2** using the Normal force. With these parameters, we will have a particle system that looks exactly like the following screenshot:

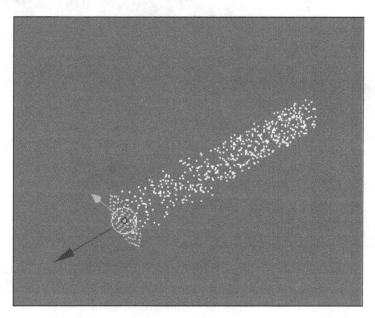

The next step is to add some rotation to the system, and to do this, we will go to the **Physics** menu and choose the random and rotation parameters. Set these parameters to **3** and **0.15**, respectively.

We will end up with particles like the ones shown in the following screenshot:

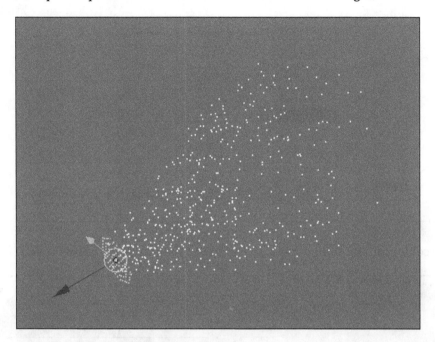

Now, go to the materials panel to set up a material to the particle system. If it doesn't have a material added to it, add one and set up the material as a halo. Here, we will use a halo with a texture to create a combustion effect to the material. Right after pressing the halo button, go to the textures panel and add a Blend texture to the object.

From the textures panel, go to the **Color** menu and turn the **Colorband** button on. With this button, we can use color gradients as textures of objects. Here are a few tips to remember when working with gradients:

- The gradient is made by a set of index colors
- Each color can be changed if its index is selected
- When the index is selected, we can change the alpha and RGB values for each of the colors

To edit and change the colors of a gradient, use the index selector, index display, alpha, and the RGB values shown in the following screenshot:

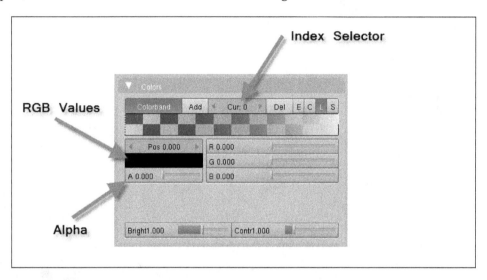

Set the color gradient until it has a nice gradient ranging from yellow to red.

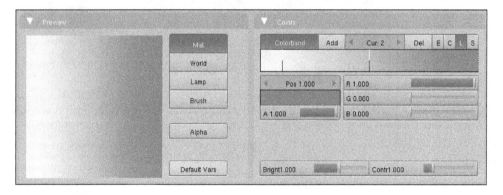

With the color gradient set up, we can go to the **Materials** panel again and adjust the halos to make our effect work like rocket combustion. Turn the **Flare** button on and add more strength to the halo with the Boost and Add sliders. The final image should look like the following screenshot:

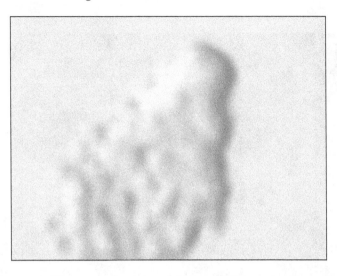

In this case, the values that have been used for the Add and Boost sliders are 0.6 and 3, respectively.

The guns

With the engine ready, we can begin working on the same effect for the guns, but with a different objective. Here, we will create something like a plasma or ray gun that will be shooting in space. The direction and treatment of the particles will be different, mostly because of the direction of the particles, which will behave like small comets rather than bursts of energy from an engine.

For the guns, our emitter will be a sphere with a reasonable amount of subdivision. Select this object and add a good amount of velocity based on their normals. To make the particles simulate the behavior of a comet, add a force in the X or Y direction of the particles to make the force change all trajectories of the particles and push them in a unique direction.

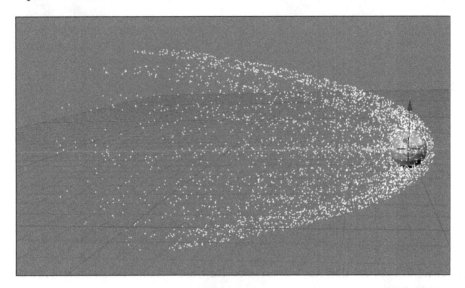

That's all we need for this particle system. The rest of the process is exactly the same as the particles of the engine. Only the color of the texture should be different and should appear greener.

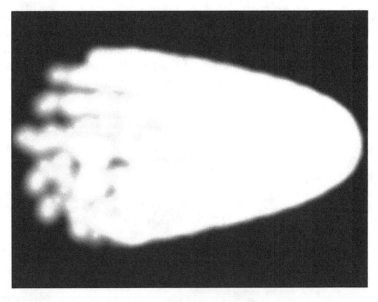

Summary

In this chapter, we added even more elements and visual aids to our project in order to bring more realism to the scene. If we use well-planned special effects for any type of object, the overall visual impact of the project can be much greater!

Here is a summary of what we have learned in this chapter:

- How to use and set up particles in Blender 3D
- How to create combustion flares with particles
- How to create plasma rays with particles

10
Rendering the Spacecraft with YafaRay

In this chapter, we will learn more about YafaRay and render your spacecraft project with it to achieve a photo-real effect from the lighting and materials. Back in the first project, we began using YafaRay to render our first project with an abstract environment called *Studio Setup*. Now, we will place the flying spacecraft in a space simulating a physical sky. Along with the rendering process of YafaRay, we will learn how to set up the environment and render the methods and materials of YafaRay.

Environment setup in YafaRay—creating a physical sky

The objective of this chapter is to show all of the steps required to set up a physical sky with YafaRay and make a realistic render with our steampunk spacecraft. Before anything, we have to open the YafaRay exporter script in the **Scripts** folder of Blender 3D. This folder was already created in Chapter 5, *Rendering the Project with YafaRay*, when we set up the render for our first Incredible Machine project. In the YafaRay exporter, we will find a tab called **World**, which is where we will find the information and tools to create a physical sky.

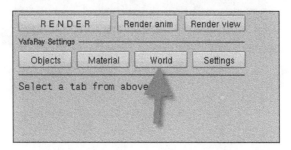

After choosing the **World** tab, a selector will appear and then we will choose one of the background types available.

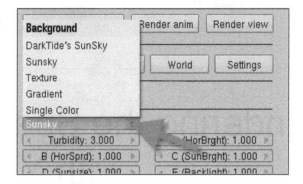

All options present different settings and effects on the scene based on the way we change the parameters from each one of them. Different backgrounds produce different effects. Let's take a look at the background types.

Single Color

Here, we will have a single color background. We have only the option to choose the background color and the **Power** value, which determines how strong the background color will be. This option is used mostly when a simple scene is required and will not produce realistic results.

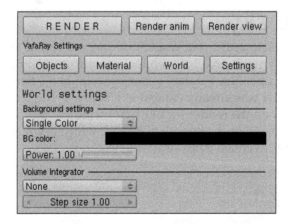

Gradient

With the gradient type, the background setup will use several colors to represent the sky. There are options to control the Horizon, Horizon color, Zenith, and Zenith color. A gradient will create a good representation of a sky, but it only reproduces the colors.

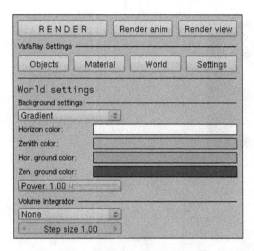

Texture

One of the ways to add realism to a scene is by using a special image called HDRI as a background texture. This type of texture looks much like a photo, but it can emit light. An **HDRI (High Dynamic Range Imaging)** looks like a spherical texture that will surround and add light energy to the scene. Besides the light energy, we will have great reflections created by the texture in materials such as metals and glass. To use this option, choose texture as a background in YafaRay and press the **Use IBL** button. **IBL** stands for **Image Based Lighting**. For this option to work, we have to add an HDR image as a background in Blender.

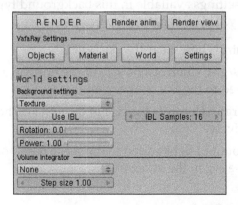

To add a texture to the background in Blender, go to the **Texture** panel and choose the **World** option.

Several HDR texture files are available to download for free at this address:
`http://www.debevec.org/probes/`

SunSky

The first option that enables us to create a physical sky with YafaRay is the SunSky background. With the settings available in this background type, our scene will reproduce a realistic sky. This is what each parameter does:

- **Turbidity**: Controls how clear the sky will be.
- **HorSprd/HorBrght**: Controls the size of the horizon gradient and the brightness related to the sky, respectively.
- **Sunsize/SunBrght**: Controls the size of the sun and how bright it will be, respectively.
- **Backlight**: Amount of light added to the scene based on the scattered light generated by the fog in the atmosphere.

- **From (get angle)/From (get position)/From (update sun)**: We can use these buttons when a sun lamp is selected in the 3D view of Blender to control the position of the sun interactively.

- **Add real sun/Skylight**: The first button adds a sun to the scene based on the settings of the background. The second one adds a skylight, adding light energy to the scene.

We can control the overall power of the background with the left **Power** slider; the right Power slider will control the sun's intensity.

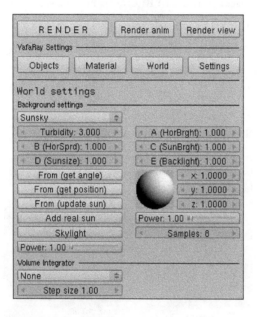

DarkTide's SunSky

This is the most complete type of background for YafaRay with settings that give us full control over the sky. One of the most interesting features of this background is that we have a **Night** button that can turn the sun into a moon, rendering a scene with a darker environment. There are several options to control the sky:

- **Turbidity**: Controls how clear or foggy the sky is. Values between 3 or 6 produce a normal day sky, and with values between 2 or 5, we have a very clear sky.

- **Solar region intensity/Width of circumsolar region**: Both values control the brightness and size of the sun.

- **Brightness of horizon gradient/Luminance of horizon**: Both settings will control the brightness of the horizon. The first one controls the brightness directly, and the second one controls the size of the horizon gradient.

- **Backscattered light**: This is the light scattered from the fog in the atmosphere. If we set the turbidity to produce a clear sky, changing this parameter won't add much light to the scene.

- **From (get angle)/From (get position)/ From (update sun)**: We can use these buttons when a sun lamp is selected in the 3D view of Blender to control the position of the sun interactively, as with the SunSky background.

- **Altitude**: Changes the Z coordinate of the background.

- **Add real sun**: Adds sun to the scene based on the settings of the background.

- **Add Skylight**: Makes the sky generate light energy.

- **Night**: Turns the sun into a moon, and all settings will be tweaked to render a night scene.

- **Power**: Controls the overall power of the background.

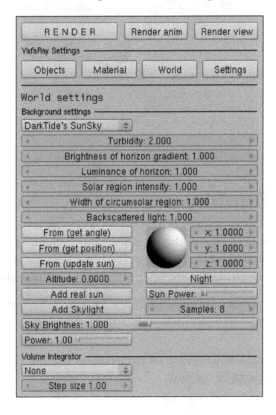

Materials and textures in YafaRay

With the background settings covered, we can begin working on the materials of the spacecraft. If the project is rendered with YafaRay, the advantage is that YafaRay uses all of the settings from the Blender materials and textures, especially if we have UV textures. In this case, UV textures are required to make image-based textures appear in YafaRay. As we have already set up this type of texture for the model, it's only a matter of choosing shades and overall settings for the object.

Let's open the **Material** tab of YafaRay and choose a material preset from the drop-down menu.

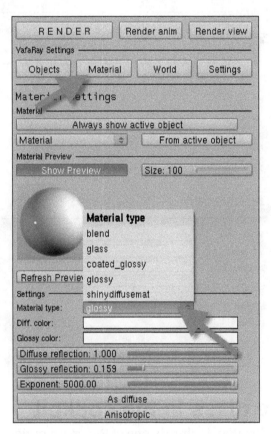

Setting up a metal material

For metal materials that reflect the environment, we can use the glossy option. First, select any part of the model that will receive a metal material such as the wings. Among all settings in this material type, we will mostly use the **Glossy reflection** and **Exponent** to create the metal. Change the **Glossy reflection** to **0.3** and the **Exponent** to **500**. The first value controls the material's level of reflectance, and the second controls how blurred the reflection will be. With an exponent of 500, we won't have a mirror effect; instead, we will have something that resembles rusted metal.

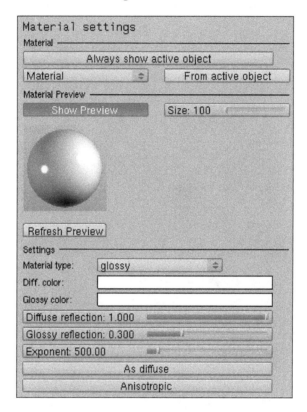

Creating the glass in the cockpit

The glass material in YafaRay is already one of the preset options that we have to change. Select the cockpit model, and choose glass as the material for YafaRay. As the interior of the spacecraft is not modeled, it would be wise to set the alpha parameter of the material to a value close to **0.8**, making it really hard to see through the glass.

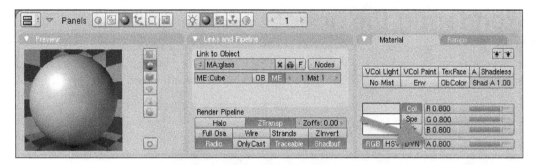

In the YafaRay material panel, choose **1.5** for the **IOR** setting to better represent the Index of Refraction of the glass. The **Absorp. color** option will be black as well to make the glass darker.

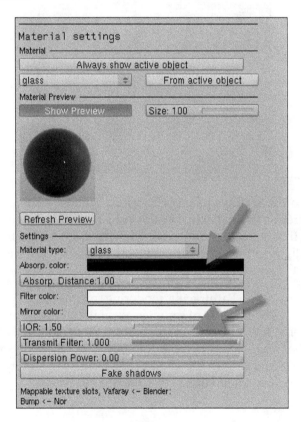

Textures and YafaRay

With YafaRay, we can use several texture slots of Blender to change the materials, like the Nor parameter to create Bump maps.

Rendering the scene

Now, it's time to render the scene and create a daylight and night render of the spacecraft. For this scene, we will use a DarkTide's SunSky background. Go to **World settings** and choose a **DarkTide's SunSky** background with the following settings:

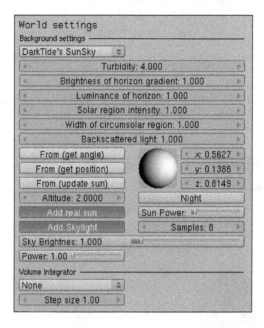

Now, go directly to the **Settings** panel of YafaRay. There we will pick a rendering method from several types available. For this project, one of the best options is Pathtracing. With this type of rendering, the light rays are traced from the camera until they reach a light source. The path made by the light source is used to calculate the light added to the scene.

To control the quality of the Pathtracing rendering, we will use a parameter called Path samples. With a low number of samples, we will have a lot of noise in the render. With higher values, the render will become clean and will also take more time to generate the image. For this project, we will use 32 samples to test the settings and 256 for the final render. Turn the **Use background** button on to add the SunSky background to the render calculation.

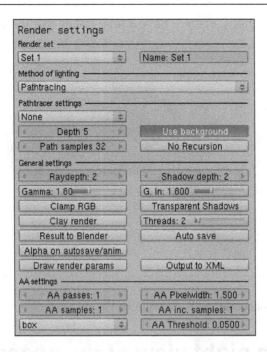

Transparent objects

For renders with a lot of transparent objects, we can use the Ray Depth and Shadow Depth option to add more interactions to the render.

The render test doesn't require a good level of anti-aliasing, and for that we can leave the **AA settings** with the default options to test. When the objective is to produce the final render, change the **AA passes** to **5**, **AA samples** to **5**, and **AA inc. samples** to **5** as well.

Using multiple threads

Choose the number of threads to use all cores from your CPU in case your computer has a processor with multi-core capabilities. This will speed up the render.

After all of the preparations, we will have a final image like the one below:

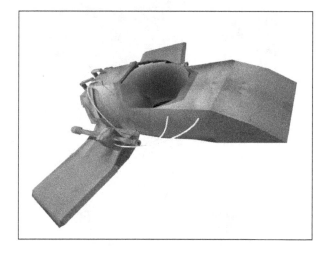

This represents the spacecraft with a daylight view.

Rendering a night view of the spacecraft

To create a night scene that represents a different view of the spacecraft, we can open the background options of YafaRay and at DarkTide's SunSky settings, and press the **Night** button. Render the image again with the same settings from the daylight view, and we will have the following image:

Summary

In this chapter, we finished the work on our second Incredible Machine. We used YafaRay to create a realistic environment and materials to render our spacecraft.

Here is a list of what we have learned in this chapter:

- How to set up physical skies with YafaRay
- How to set up backgrounds in YafaRay
- How to use HDR images as scene backgrounds in Blender 3D and YafaRay
- How to set up materials in YafaRay
- How to render daylight and night simulations with YafaRay

11
Transforming Robot

In this chapter, we will finally begin working on the last Incredible Machine, which will be, of course, the most complex and difficult project of them all. The title of the project will be **Transforming Robot** and, as you can imagine, it will be about a robot that can transform its shape into something else.

What is a transforming robot?

For this chapter, I have picked an object that represents a real challenge for any 3D artist—a complex robot that changes its shape and transforms itself into another object. Both objects that we have modeled in the previous chapters have their own difficulties and challenges, but this one will be the real modeling and animation challenge.

In a project that deals with a vehicle or object that walks around, we only have to worry about the movement of one object and set up the parenting of the model to fit only one dynamics. As it's a compound object, the modeling will actually be a double-sized project, and we will have to think about two models of the same type during the modeling. Otherwise, the transformation and animation in which the robot turns into a vehicle won't work out later.

How big will the robot be?

We can't push too much on the size of the robot to be able to actually finish the project within a single book, so the robot will be a mid-sized one. Don't expect something like a robot turning into a truck because it would require an enormous level of detail. Our project will be just enough for you to start your own transforming robot.

For this project, we will pick a robot that has a simple shape, can be modeled easily in Blender, and can transform into part of a sci-fi scenario. It doesn't mean that the vehicle won't have any details like individual light spots; it only means that we will finish the model and learn the full modeling and animation process!

Besides the model, we will also work on the scenario in which the robot will be presented. To make a really great rendering from our robot, we will create a sci-fi scenario for the robot. This will allow us to create something close to a game set, where the robot will be placed for combat or hidden among other objects.

As you can imagine, this project will take this object and break it into several parts that can be turned into a robot. As this robot has a more geometrical shape and fewer removable parts, the most important task before we start to work on the modeling is to define when and where we will break the topology.

Textures and materials

The challenges of this project don't stop with the end of all modeling because we will still have to work with textures and materials for this robot. Working with such metallic surfaces will demand a good blend of textures and materials, especially if we want to use a robot that has an old look. When I say old, I mean something that has already engaged in battle and has some scars in its paint.

If your textures aren't ready, a bit of work on GIMP or another graphical editor will help a lot with the process.

Rendering with LuxRender

In the first two projects of the book, we used YafaRay to add extra realism to the project by using advanced lighting and materials. For the robot project, we will also use advanced ray tracing techniques, but not with YafaRay. The render engine that we will be using for the robot is called LuxRender, and it's another powerful option we use to create realistic images with Blender 3D.

LuxRender is a render engine that uses unbiased methods to calculate light, which means it's physically based. All light interactions and effects are based on real interactions, which makes it easy for us to produce realistic images. For this project, we will learn how to install and set up materials and lights to render with LuxRender.

A great feature of LuxRender, as compared to YafaRay, is the ability to pause and resume the render at any time. The rendered solution is saved to a file and can even resume the render in another computer.

Mixing modeling and animation

The modeling of the third Incredible Machine is only a small part of the challenge that we will be facing ahead, and right after the model is created, we will dive into animation. Working with the animation of such a complex and exotic model will require extra care during the setup process. We'll have an object that behaves like a static object some moments and then turns into a humanoid character with arms and legs. To create this type of animation, we will have to learn some animation features of Blender, like the setup of armatures and hierarchies, as well as controllers.

For an artist specializing in modeling, working with animation can be quite a challenge because he/she will have to worry about another dimension for our models, which is timing. As the use of timing is not that easy and can't be learned overnight, you will have to be patient and practice a lot to get the right animations.

Modeling the object with poly modeling

For modeling our last Incredible Machine, we will start by placing a reference image in the background of our 3D view. If you don't want to follow the next chapters by using the image that I will be using, feel free to choose another image or technical view of the object. In fact, if you want to make another object, it's only a matter of finding the right images to start a different model. That's the great part about following a guide—you can learn the basics and then start making your own projects with the acquired knowledge. The image that I will be using can be downloaded from Packt Publishing's website, along with some other images and the final project file.

The first thing to do is place the image in the background, and to do that, we will use the **View** menu and choose **Background image**. When the small menu appears, choose the image and use the controls and options to align and place the image in the best position. As we've done the same adjustment in previous chapters, I believe there should be no problem in placing the image in the background using the same techniques as before.

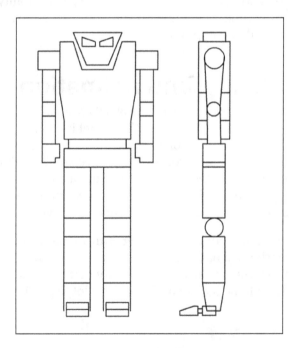

With the image in the background, we will start the modeling process, which will be based on a mix of poly modeling and subdivision modeling.

Choosing a modeling technique

For projects like this, we can choose between the following two modeling techniques that work with Blender:

- Poly modeling
- Subdivision modeling

The subdivision modeling is done by adding a cube or another 3D primitive and cutting and adjusting this model progressively to get to the shape of the vehicle. With poly modeling, we would add a simple plane and with that single plane, the process will go on by selecting and extruding edges of the plane until we get the shape of the model. Each process has pros and cons. Using subdivision, the model can be created much faster but with a low level of detail.

Working with details in subdivision modeling can be a hard task sometimes because we have to add edge loops and new edges to an already created topology.

On the other side, by using the poly modeling technique, we will add the topology on the fly, while we are still modeling the vehicle. So, it will be much easier to create and adjust details to the model by using poly modeling.

In this project, we will use a blended technique, with some parts of the object created with poly modeling and another part with subdivision.

Polygons in Blender

Blender cannot create polygons with more than four edges, and because of that, we will have to be careful about the way we create the topology of the model. This type of face with more than four sides is called an N-Gon. There is a project to add support to N-Gons in Blender 3D, called B-Mesh. However, as it's a work in progress and there is no release date, we will have to stick with three and four-sided polys.

Modeling the legs

With the images and modeling technique defined, we can start working on the model. Place the camera in front view, or choose a view that gives the best visualization for the side of the object. As this is a perfectly symmetrical model, we will start modeling half of the model and later create a mirrored copy.

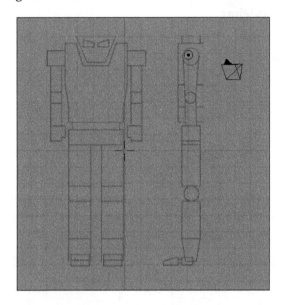

At first, the model may look simple and without details, but in Chapter 13, *Making the Robot Look Metallic with Materials in LuxRender*, we will add a few details to the model and create a scenario in which to add the robot. With LuxRender materials, the model will gain an incredible look and realism at the rendering.

To begin modeling the legs, we will add a cube to the scene and make a few transformations. First, select just one of the sides for the cube and move it. Use a scale transformation to fit the cube in the reference image.

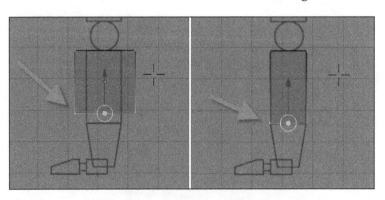

When the extrusion is created, change the selection mode to edge, select only the two edges pointed in the following image, and apply two extrusions:

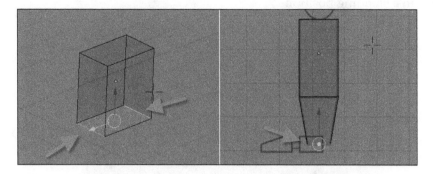

Now, change the work mode to object and add another cube. Scale and move the cube down until it fits the small area created in the previous step.

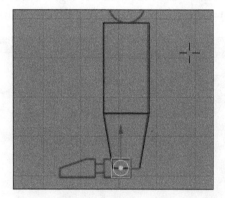

Enter in edit mode, and with a set of extrusions and transformations, make the cube look like the following image. It's just a series of extrusions and scale transformations; we have already used the same technique in the spacecraft project. The cube will be used as the foot of the robot.

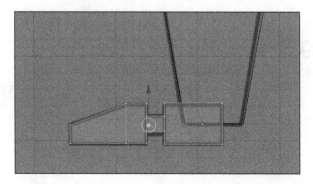

Now, we will add a cylinder to be used as a knee for the robot. Add a cylinder and scale it down until it looks like the following image. Notice that we are modeling the robot in a standing position.

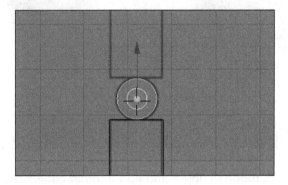

To finish the modeling for the base model of the leg, we will add another cube and set it until it looks like the following image. It's a simple scale transformation.

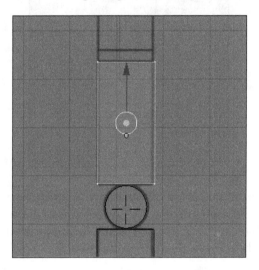

Modeling the main body

The next part that we will model is the main body of the robot, which is made by three cubes. These cubes will articulate and connect the lower and upper parts of the model, like the arms and legs. To get started, add a simple cube to the scene and deform it until the object fits the reference image.

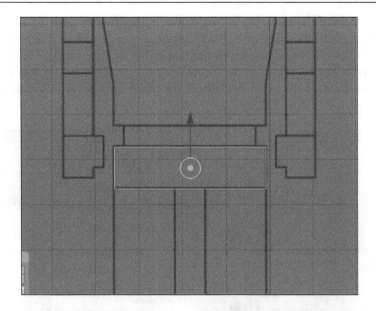

In object mode, select the cube and duplicate it to create the second part of the main body. Add a **Bevel** modifier with the default settings to both cubes in order to add a chamfer to all edges of the cubes.

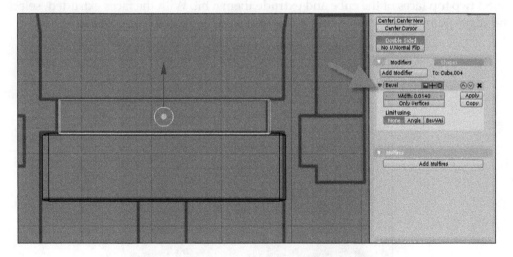

For the upper part of the main body, we will need another cube with a few extra transformations. Add the cube and in edit mode, press the *Ctrl+R* keys to add a face loop cut in the direction shown in the image below (section 1). Create two cuts by pressing the + key on the numeric keyboard or by rolling the mouse scroll. After that, add another cut in the middle of the object at a perpendicular direction (section 2).

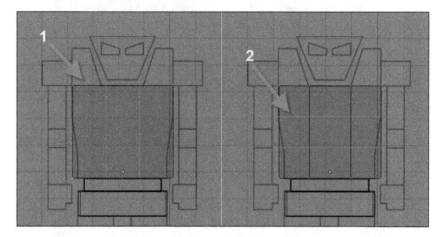

Select two top faces of the cube and extrude them a bit. With the faces extruded, select the edges pointed in the following image and scale them in the opposite direction:

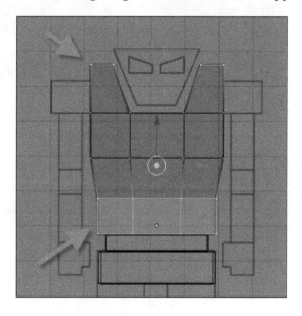

Modeling the head

The head of the model will be made by a cube as well, but with a few additions and changes to create a set of eyes that emit light. We will use a feature of LuxRender that uses mesh objects to emit light energy, and it will produce a nice glowing eyes effect. To start the modeling, add a cube to the scene and in edit mode with a face loop cut, add a new edge loop in the center of the cube. Select just half of the model and erase the vertices, adjusting the remaining objects to fit the reference image.

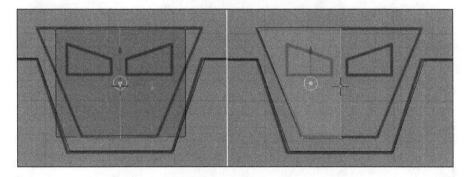

With the face loop cut, add the following edge loops to the object:

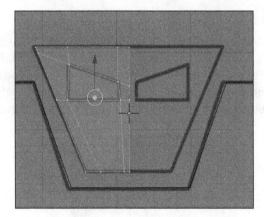

With two extrusions, create the shape of the eye, and finish the head with a mirror modifier.

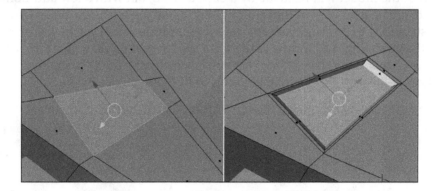

Mirror center

If the mirror modifier creates the copy of the object in the wrong place, check the center of the object.

Modeling the arms

The arms will be created with a few primitive shapes as well, just like the rest of the robot body. It will be exactly three cubes and two cylinders. Both cylinders are created with the default options but scaled down to fit in the shoulder and elbow. For the arm and forearm, we will also use two default cubes with a scale transformation applied to make the object look like the following image:

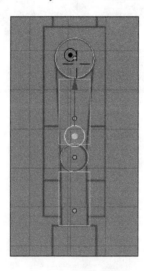

For the hand, we will add a few extra transformations. Add a cube and, while in edit mode, select the face pointed in the following image and extrude it once. When the first extrusion is created, select the other face pointed and extrude it again:

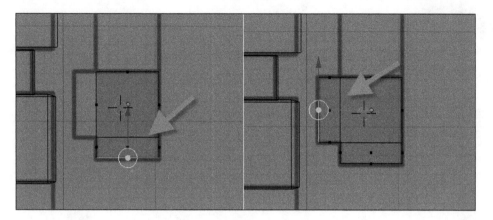

Summary

In this chapter, we had a brief overview of the last Incredible Machine that we will be creating in Blender. As part of the book sequence, the project will deal with more objects, complex data, and relations between 3D objects.

Here is a list of things that we have learned in this chapter:

- What a transforming robot is
- What our last Incredible Machine is
- The challenges involved in the project
- How to create the base model
- The differences between poly and subdivision modeling
- What LuxRender is

12
Using Modifiers and Curves to Create Details for the Robot and Scene

In the last chapter, we started creating our robot and gave it a rough form using a bunch of polygons and a reference image. The robot was incomplete at the end of Chapter 11, so now we will continue the modeling process by using some modifiers and curves turned into 3D meshes to add more detail to the overall model. In addition, we will start creating the scenario used to create the robot in LuxRender using a few tricks and special materials to give it a sci-fi look.

Modifiers

Blender has a lot of modifiers that can really improve the modeling process, and we will be using some of them to add a few details and improve the modeling. Before we use these modifiers directly, let's take a quick look at how each of the modifiers work and how they can help us. Some of them are new to Blender, so if you don't know them yet, here's a chance to learn about them.

Here are some of the modifiers that we will be using:

- **Bevel**: With this modifier, we can chamfer and fillet the edges of a model. This is quite important for realism because in the real world, we don't have perfect edges. For most of the model, we will add a small level of bevel.

- **Array**: The array modifier is a common tool for 3D software, and it's responsible for the creation of duplicates sometimes using a 3D matrix or curves. For our project, it will be useful to create grids and other elements that repeat themselves over the surfaces.

- **Mesh Deform**: This is a relatively new modifier in Blender that is used for animation. With this tool, we can deform objects and meshes using some sort of cage. It will also be good for animation and modeling because we will also be able to bend and adjust the shape of all parts of the robot.

- **Simple Deform**: Here, we have a new modifier in Blender. Its function is to add simple deformations to objects like bend, stretch, twist, and taper. As it's a lot easier to deform objects using this modifier, every time our model requires something similar to a simple deform, we will use it.

Some artists don't like to use modifiers to model much because they lose some control over the object, leaving the creation of geometry to the modifiers. However, the great advantage of using modifiers is that you can organize them in the modifier stack. At any time, we can move, swap the order of the modifiers, and erase them.

There are some tools in Blender that aren't classified as modifiers, but when we apply the tool to some object, a new modifier is listed in the modifier stack. For instance, if we add a hook to any type of object, it will be listed as a modifier. We will be using some of those tools as well, and we will edit them with the modifier menu.

Using the bevel modifier to chamfer the edges of the model

Let's get started with the most simple of the modifiers, which is the Bevel. As stated earlier in the chapter, the bevel modifier can add a chamfer to the edges of the model and also create a filled corner. The bevel modifier works using a property of the edges called **Bevel Weight**. To use this modifier in only some edges of the model, we first have to set the bevel weight.

To set the bevel weight, we can use a keyboard short cut, which is *Ctrl+Shift+E*, or we can use the **Mesh** menu. Just go to the edge options and you will find the **Bevel Weight**.

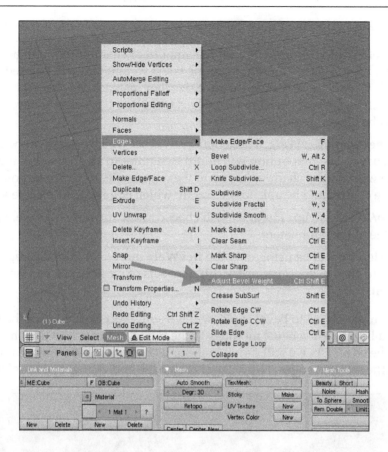

Bevel weight is just a way to add different values to the edges of an object and make chamfers with distinct intensities. If you can't visualize the differences or values for the bevel weight, the property can be adjusted later. Add a modifier to the object, and choose **Bevel** from the modifier list.

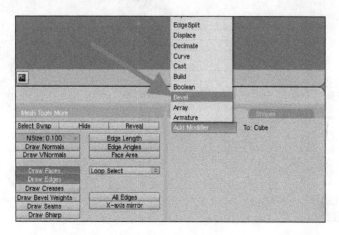

Here is a brief description of how the most important parameters of the bevel work:

- **Bevel Width**: Here, we will set the amount of chamfer that will be applied to each edge. This is different from the bevel weight and will be used together with the weight to set the chamfer size. For instance, if we set the width to 0.5 and the weight of two different edges to 0.2 and 0.8, respectively, the chamfer will be bigger in the second edge.

- **None/Angle/BevWeig**: These options will set which edges will be used for the bevel. The first option will add the chamfer to all edges, and the second one will create a chamfer based on the edge angle. With the last one, we will have control and be able to set exactly which edge should receive a chamfer.

- **Min/Average/Max**: Here, we will choose to use the min, average, or max value of the parameters.

For our model, we will be using only the **BevWeig** button and the **Average** option. If you want to change anything or try different sets of parameters, feel free to modify them.

With everything related to bevel explained, we will select each edge of the model and apply a bevel. Add a bevel modifier to the model, and set it to use only the bevel weight of the edges. As we still didn't make any changes to the weights, nothing will happen to the selected edges. Now, select each edge and change the bevel weight.

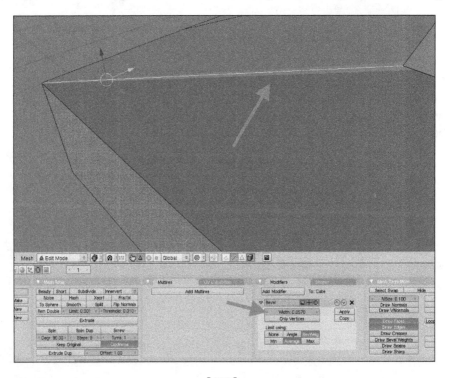

If everything was changed correctly, we will see a chamfer in each edge. If you really want the model to display a great level of realism, add a small chamfer to all edges of the model. The amount should be really small, only enough to make the chamfer visible at rendering.

Only with this setting, we can add a lot of geometry to the object without adding new geometry to the model, which is great in animation.

Using the array modifier to add rivets

The full structure of the robot is welded and connected using rivets, which could be represented with textures or image maps, and in some cases, using real objects. It would be great if we could represent the rivets only with textures, but at some point of the project, we will create animations that will get the camera really close to the robot. So, if we don't want to get a poor visualization of this kind of detail, the best option is to use geometry.

The array modifier is a great option to distribute the rivets over the surface because we can use options to create copies of the geometry using large sets of parameters. Before going to the array modifier menu, create a mesh circle with twelve sides to use as a rivet model. Apply an extrusion to this circle model to make it look like the following image:

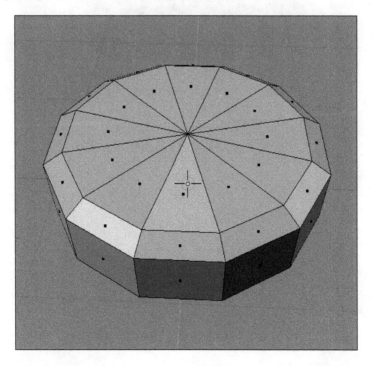

Now, with the object selected, we can add an array modifier and set it to distribute the object over a surface. The array modifier can be used to copy objects using a matrix as a reference, and for each level of rivets, we will add a new modifier.

For instance, here is an example of a rivet set made by two lines and five columns. To create this type of object, we have to add one array for each line or column.

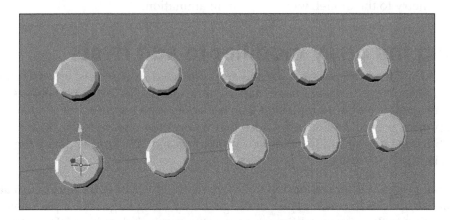

This is what the array modifier will look like for this object:

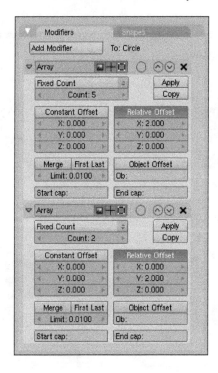

If we have more lines or columns of objects, we will need more modifiers. Using two arrays is necessary because the array adds objects using a matrix as a reference, and for each column or line of the matrix, we will need a new array.

Follow the reference image and create all sets of rivets for the model. When we start creating the animation, we will have to find a way for the rivet objects to follow the movements of other elements. This will be created with the use of hierarchies. Select the objects created by the array modifier, and parent them to the robot model. Simply press *Ctrl+P* when they are selected.

Creating wires and cables with curves and hooks

We have already used curves to create wires for our second Incredible Machine, and now we will create a few more wires and cables. This time, the cables and wires will only appear when the robot is turned into the human form. A quick look at the image presented in the previous chapter will show that the robot only shows cables in the human form.

Create a Bezier curve, and turn it into a vector curve by pressing the *V* key when both control points of the curve are selected (while you are still in edit mode).

Now, create a Bezier circle right next to the curve. With all vertices of the circle selected, duplicate the object with the *Shift+D* key. A set of three new circles will be enough for this type of object. Select the Bezier curve, and set the BevOb property of the curve with the name of the circle. This will create an object similar to the one created for the spacecraft.

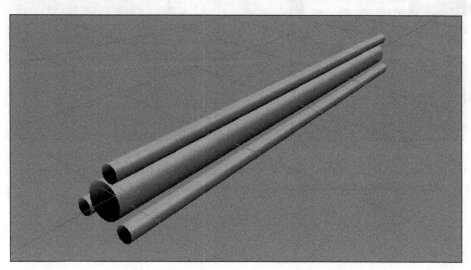

The difference now is that we will have to add controls to deform the cables during animation. This can be achieved by using an object that we haven't used so far, called **Hooks**. The hooks work like the name implies, pushing and pulling vertexes. Besides the animation features of the hooks, they are a great way to control different curves without having to enter in edit mode for each object.

Follow these steps to add a hook to a curve:

1. Select a control point of the curve.
2. Press the *Ctrl+H* key.
3. Choose **Add, New Empty**.

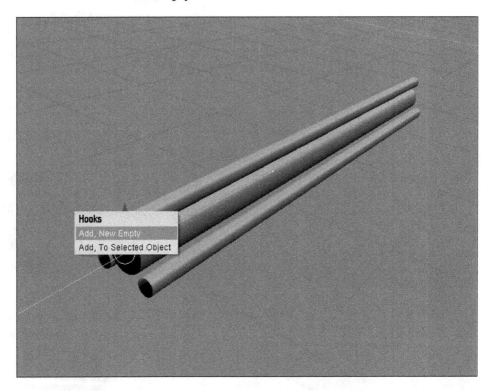

By doing that, we will create a new **Empty** connected to the control point of the curve, and by moving the empty object, we will deform the curve.

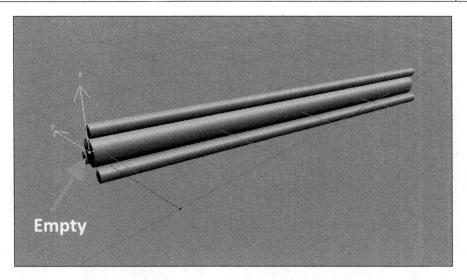

Every time we add a new hook to an object, a new modifier will be added to the stack. As you can see, for each hook, a new modifier is created.

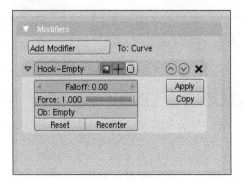

By using the modifier stack, we can control and erase the hook from any type of object. Though it is not a modifier, the hook tool is treated like one after we use it in some objects. The best part of working with hooks is that we can add keyframes to them and deform the object with animated moves.

To finish the creation of the cables, turn the 3D button in the editing panel of the curve on. Select one of the control points of the curve, and press the *T* key to enable the tilt tool on. Move the mouse to twist the curve and produce a more realistic cable.

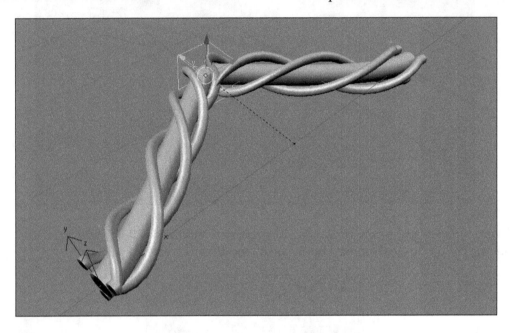

Adding details to the robot

Now, let's make a few changes to the robot model. Select the upper part of the leg and add a few subdivisions. This process is identical to the one used in the first two projects, where we added a circular hole to a 3D mesh. If you don't remember the process, select a face and erase it, and at the same place where the face was, add a mesh circle.

First add a new edge loop to the cube that represents the upper part of the leg, as shown in the following image (section 1). Then, add another set of five edge loops to the model (section 2).

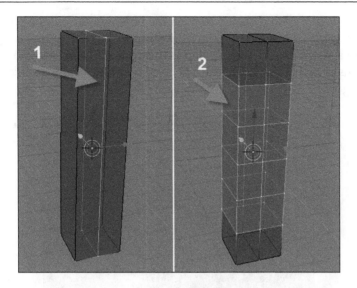

With the edge loops added, select the four center faces of the model and erase the face (section 1). Align the 3D cursor at the center of the hole opened, and add a mesh circle in a view perpendicular to the hole. The circle must have exactly eight vertices (section 2).

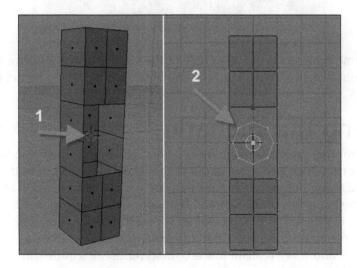

When the circle is placed and scaled to fit in the hole, we can fill the space with faces using the *Shift+F* keys. Or, we can select four vertices at a time and press the *F* key to create a single face. The next step is to add a series of extrusions and scale transformations to create the spotlight. The final result should look like the following image:

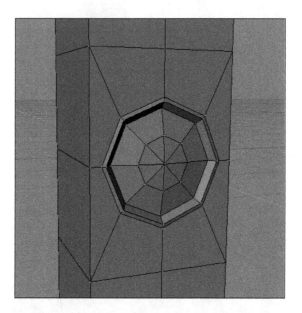

Repeat the same process for the other side of the leg. Try using a mirror modifier this time. To do this, however, we would have to erase half of the leg model first.

Modeling the scenario

The scenario for this project is made from a set of walls and a few objects distributed around the scene, which add more detail to the composition. Most of the scenario will be created using poly modeling techniques, such as the extrusion of edges. A few objects (the big boxes of the set) will be made with subdivision modeling. One thing to notice in this scenario composition is that it's made up of simple objects. Even with simple objects, the repetition of elements in scenes like the one we are working on will add more realism to the overall render. It's quite different from the studio setup that we worked on in the past two projects.

To begin the modeling of the scenario, we will add the walls and floor of the set. Add a mesh plane to the scene and scale it up. If the model looks much different from the scale of the robot, we can always change the scale of the set later.

With the plane positioned, we will add a series of cuts and extrusions to create the full set. First, select both edges pointed in the following image, and extrude them in the Z axis (section 1). Then, add a face loop cut with two divisions (section 2).

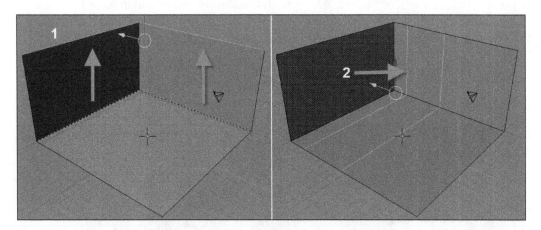

Next, add another loop cut, select the face pointed in the following image (section 1), and create an extrusion at the back of the face. This will create a hallway in the scenario (section 2).

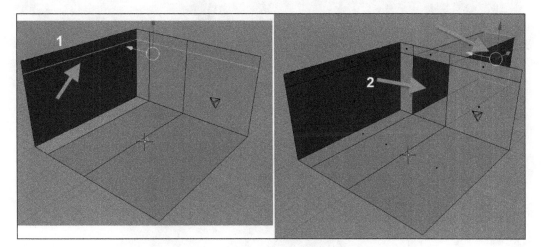

Modeling the stands for the robots

Besides the walls of the set, we have to model the places where the robot models, in compact form, will be stored. Along with the stands, we will also have to create a few pillars for the structure of the model. If we take a look at the image shown in the previous chapter, we will also have a luminary attached to the pillar.

Start with a mesh cube creation, and scale it up in the Z axis to make it look like the following image (section 1). Select the top face of the cube, and extrude it up a bit in the Z axis again (section 2).

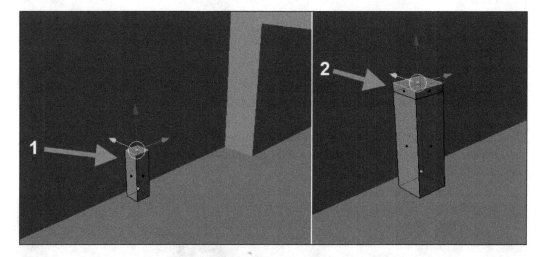

Now, select one of the small faces created with the last extrusion (pointed in the following image), and extrude it to the left.

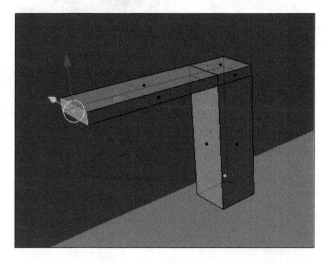

This is the base model for the stand, which can be distributed in the scene using an array modifier. Add the modifier and set it to create three copies of the object in the Z axis. After that, add another array to create three more copies of the stand in the X axis.

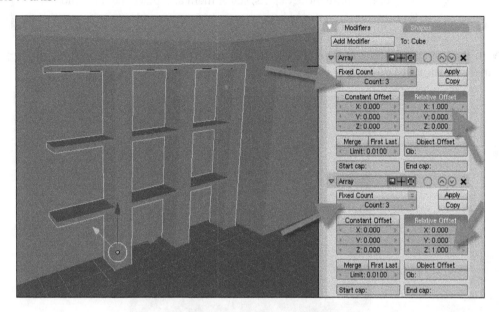

Creating the storage boxes

The scenario is filled with a few storage boxes made out of a metallic material. By now, we won't have to create any materials or textures in the objects, but we will model the structure of the box to apply the materials later. The storage box is based on a deformed plane, created with a common subdivision modeling technique. To start the modeling of the box, add a mesh plane to the 3D view, and extrude it six times as shown in the following image. Try to follow the same proportions presented in the image.

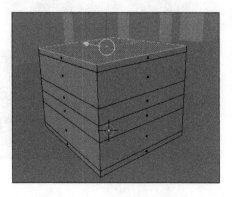

[
Hidden objects

By now, we may have lots of objects in 3D view. If you want to temporarily hide those objects, select them and place them on another layer by pressing the *M* key.
]

With the extruded plane still selected, we will add another set of extrusions and scale transformations to create the top of the box.

Select the edge loops pointed out in the following image by either making a box selection with the *B* key or by right-clicking and pressing the *Alt* key. When the edge loops are selected, scale them down to fit the shape presented in the following image:

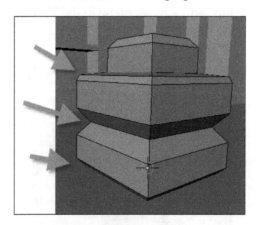

To finish the creation of the box, we will now add a bevel modifier to create a chamfer on all edges of the model. Use a value of 0.05 for the bevel.

Modeling lights

For this project in particular, we will have to work with area lights. Blender 3D works with point light sources that aren't supported by LuxRender. For LuxRender we have to use area lights, which may be planes or objects that emit light energy. We will add the light sources now, and we will set the materials and light emission details in a later chapter. For our scene, there are three types of light sources:

1. Area lights created by mesh planes.
2. The eyes and legs of the robots.
3. The individual light emitter, placed on the walls and floor of the scenario.

One of those light emitters is already created, which is the eyes and legs of the robot. We must create the lights on walls and the mesh planes that will distribute the energy on the scene. The planes are really simple to create, and the only work that we'll have is the distribution of the planes along the scenario.

With the lights on the walls and floor, use the same process as the one to create the circular holes on the leg of the robot. This is the procedure:

1. Create a mesh cube.
2. With all objects selected, add a subdivision to it with the *W* key.
3. Select the four faces at one side of the cube and erase them.
4. Align the 3D cursor to the hole, and create a mesh circle aligned to the cube.
5. Connect the vertices of the cube and circle to create the hole.

To finish the modeling of the object, add a few extrusions and scale transformations to make the circle look like the following image:

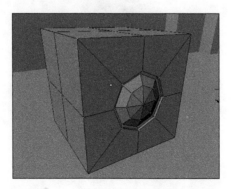

This is not the last step of the modeling for this project because we still have to create the other version of the robot to distribute it along the scenario. In the next chapter, we will work on tasks directly related to LuxRender and the setup of the scene using materials that add more realism.

Summary

In this chapter, we learned how to work with some modifiers in Blender to add more detail to the robot model. Some of those modifiers are simple to use, but they can really help to improve the model without adding new geometry. We learned how to deal with hooks, which aren't modifiers but will always be added to the modifier stack when applied to an object.

Here is a list of subjects that we have learned in this chapter:

- How to add details to objects using modifiers
- How to work with the bevel, array, and simple deform modifiers
- The importance of adding chamfered edges to models
- How to add hooks to vertices
- How to deform curves by using hooks
- How to create and connect objects with the array modifier
- How to add deformations with the simple deform modifier

13
Making the Robot Look Metallic with Materials in LuxRender

In the first two chapters of this third project, we started adding objects and details to our robot. Now, it's time to assemble all the parts of the robot and finally begin adding materials to the model in **LuxRender**. In this chapter, we will learn how to install LuxRender and export our scenes to the renderer.

Installing LuxRender

Before we go any further, we will have to install LuxRender to set up the materials of the robot model. This is necessary because LuxRender works more independently than YafaRay. If we choose to use LuxRender materials, all of them must be set up in the exporter. To use LuxRender, visit http://www.luxrender.net and download the most recent version of the renderer, which is version 0.6.

Downloads are available for Windows, Linux and Mac OS X. With the download of the LuxRender package, the Blender 3D exporter is already packed together with the installer. If you have trouble installing the exporter, the Python script called **LuxBlender** is available as a separate download. Download the file and copy it to the Blender 3D scripts folder. If you are using Blender 3D 2.49, it is necessary to install Python 2.6.x (http://www.python.org) to use LuxBlender without any errors.

During the installation process of LuxRender, the installer will ask for the location of the Blender 3D script folder, as shown in the following screenshot. (The installation is running on Windows.)

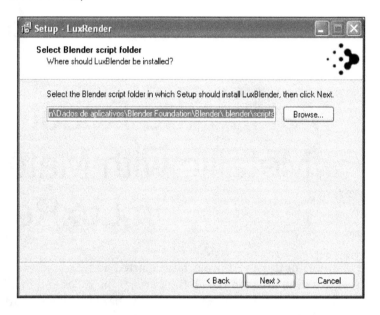

The process is pretty straightforward, and by the end, we will have the LuxRender option available in the **Render** folder of the Blender scripts window.

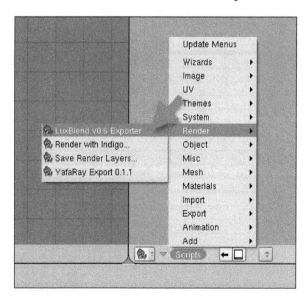

This part works in the same way as YafaRay, where we must create a division on the Blender interface to work properly with the **LuxBlend** exporter, which is the name of the tool that converts the Blender 3D file to a format that is compatible with LuxRender.

Using LuxBlend

The LuxBlend interface is organized in a similar way to the YafaRay exporter, with several tabs separating the options of the renderer. There are five fields to choose from and several presets. The large number of presets is a great resource for beginners because it allows us to use quick setups for rendering. The following screenshot shows a view of LuxBlend and its tabs:

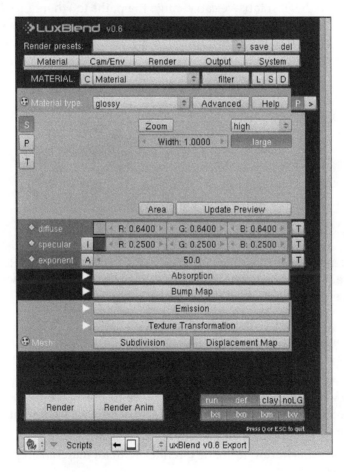

Here is what each tab does:

- **Material**: As the label of the tab says, this is where we will set up all materials related to LuxRender.

- **Cam/Env**: Here are the options to set up the environment and cameras in LuxRender. For instance, we can change the way a camera behaves or add a physical sky to the background.

- **Render**: In this tab, we find options to change the sampler used for rendering and aliasing filters.

- **Output**: Here we find options to change the resolution of the rendered image, file type used for output, and tonemapper used for rendering.

- **System**: In this last tab, we can change the paths to where LuxRender is installed and where the files generated by the renderer will be saved. This tab allows us to change the number of threads used for rendering and sets up network rendering, too.

At the bottom of LuxBlend, we find controls to export the scene to the renderer.

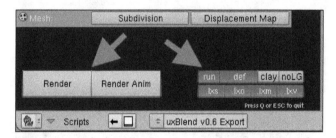

By using the Render button, we start the rendering process with LuxRender. For animations, we hit **Render Anim**. There are a few extra buttons that set how the exporter will generate all of the required files to use with LuxRender. Here is what each one of them does:

- **run**: If this button is pressed, the renderer will be automatically launched when we hit the **Render** button. The default option is to leave it on.

- **def**: Every time we start a render with Lux, the scene is exported to a file format with an .lxs extension. If this button is turned on, our scene will be saved as default.lxs. It is the directory pointed as default in the **System** tab.

- **clay**: Press this button to create a render with all materials represented as a white matte color.

- **noLG**: Here we can disable the use of light groups in the rendering.

At the bottom of the exporter we will find options to generate different file types, and pressing each one of them will mean that another file will be generated when we hit render:

- **.lxs**: LuxRender scene
- **.lxo**: LuxRender mesh objects
- **.lxm**: LuxRender materials
- **.lxv**: LuxRender volume file

By default, we leave all options enabled to generate the files.

Setting up materials for the robot

The robot model has a metallic and shiny material, very similar to gold or bronze. To set up materials in LuxBlend, select the object in which the material shall be applied. An important thing to do before we go to LuxBlend is to make sure that the object already has a material created and assigned in Blender 3D. The settings of the materials won't be used by LuxRender, but the name and identification will be.

Select any part of the robot model that should look like metal, and apply a material in Blender 3D. Assign a name to this material, such as **gold_metal**, to easily identify it in LuxBlend.

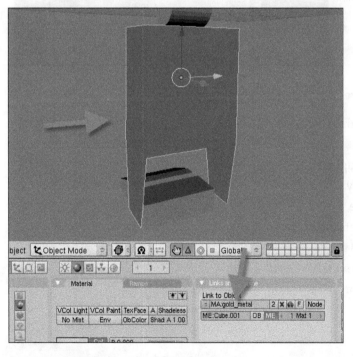

When the material is created, select the object, open LuxBlend, and click on the **Material** tab. There we will find the options to set up the material. At the top of the interface, we will see the material name, which is being edited (see pointer 1 in the following image). Just below this option, we have the material preset type (see pointer 2 in the following image). This is one of the most important selections that must be done in the materials panel.

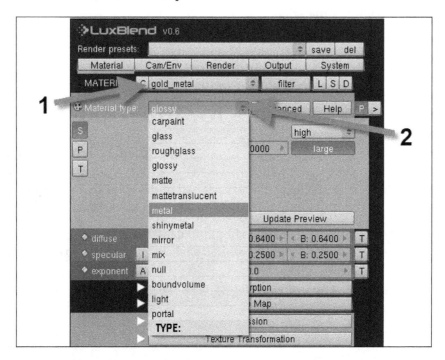

There are several types of materials available:

- carpaint
- glass
- roughglass
- glossy
- matte
- mattetranslucent
- metal
- shinymetal
- mirror
- mix
- null

- boundvolume
- light
- portal

For this project, we will use the **metal**, **matte**, **shinymetal**, and **light**. A great way to start with ready-to-use materials is by
using the LuxRender material database. We can visit and download ready-to-use materials there and load the file into our projects. To download the database, visit
`http://www.luxrender.net/lrmdb/en` and pick any material.

To load a material in LuxBlend, just click on the small arrow located at the top-right side of the LuxBlend interface and choose **Load LBM**. If you know the material ID from the database, then it's possible to directly download the material and save your own set of materials with the **Save LBM** option.

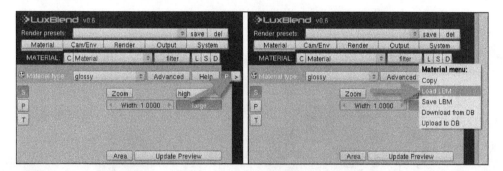

For our robot project, we will start with a metal material. Choose this type of material, and pick a metal type from the presets. In this case, we will choose gold.

This metal will work fine with an exponent of 50, which is the default value. High values of the exponent make the metal more reflective, resembling a mirror. The following screenshot shows a comparison with the **gold** material set with an exponent of **50** and **1000**.

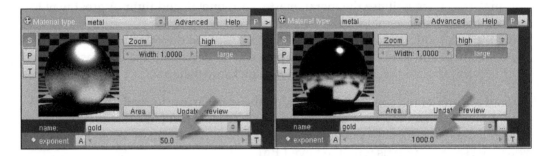

To test and see what the material will look like, change the settings of any material and click on the **Update Preview** button.

Select all other parts of the robot, and assign the same material to it.

Use the same material for the light model we created in the previous chapter. To add the material to the light model, we will separate the metal material from the spot used to add light energy to the scene. Select the light model in edit mode, press the *P* key, and choose **Selected**. This will split the 3D model into two different objects.

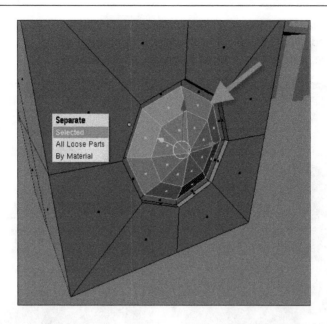

Now, select all other parts of the robot model, leaving only the eyes and the small spots on the sides of the leg unselected. They will be used as light sources in the next chapter.

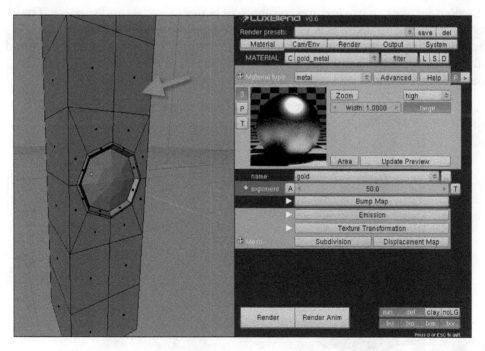

The next object that will receive a material is the box placed at the scene. With the object selected, add a material in Blender and name it **metal_aluminum**. In LuxBlend, set the material as a **metal** and choose **aluminum**.

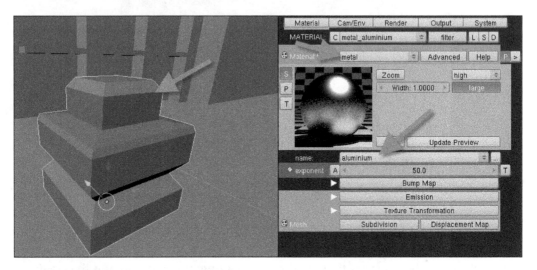

Adding textures to the ground of the scene

In LuxRender, we can use textures to represent better materials and surfaces. The process of setting up textures is very similar to YafaRay, where we have to use UV mapping to display the textures in LuxRender. To apply UV mapping to the ground of the scene, we will separate the ground from the rest of the model. Select only the faces of the ground and press the *P* key in edit mode to split the object in two.

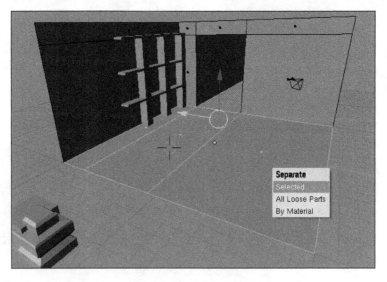

With the faces of the ground separated, we can easily add a UV map and apply a texture to the ground. Name the material **ground_texture**.

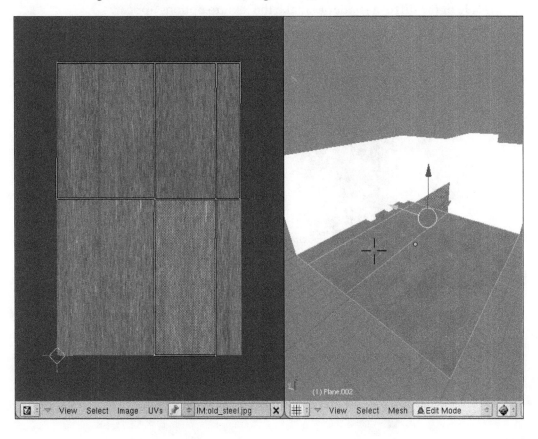

In LuxBlend, we have to select the material type as glossy and point the use of a texture in the field pointed out in the following screenshot. Press the small **T** button on the side of the **diffuse shader** to make the texture options appear.

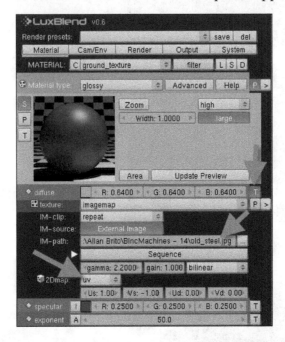

It's quite important to mark the use of a UV map in the distribution of the texture. To make sure that the texture is correctly displayed, we also have to point the path to the texture file used in the Blender material and UV mapping.

Summary

In this chapter, we added some materials and textures directly from the LuxBlend exporter interface. This allowed us to render the scene later with the LuxRender advanced render options. It was the first time we started working with LuxRender in this book as well.

Here is a list of things that we have learned in this chapter:

- How to install LuxRender
- How LuxBlend is organized
- How to set up the basic parameters of LuxRender materials
- How to choose from several preset materials of LuxRender
- How to add textures to 3D models in order for LuxRender to recognize the material

14

Adding Lights to the Scene and Rendering with LuxRender

In the previous chapters, we managed to create a model and added a few textures and materials to make it look like an old military vehicle. The next step in order to create our third Incredible Machine is to work with lights and effects, to make the light interact with the materials and textures to give reflections, and to create other illumination effects.

Unbiased render engine—how it works

An unbiased render engine is becoming very popular among 3D artists these days, but a lot of users still get confused by the way those render engines work. Before we go any further, let's take a look at how this render works to avoid any surprises. Almost all render engines today work with the so-called render threads. Render threads are small squares that render and generate the images for each sector of the image. This is the way in which almost all renderers, including the internal renderers of 3D suites such as Blender, work.

With the unbiased render engines, we will have a very different process, which uses what is called a progressive refinement of the images. By the time you hit the **Render** button, in a few moments, we will be able to see the full image of the scene. This image will have a very poor quality and a lot of noise, as shown in the following screenshot:

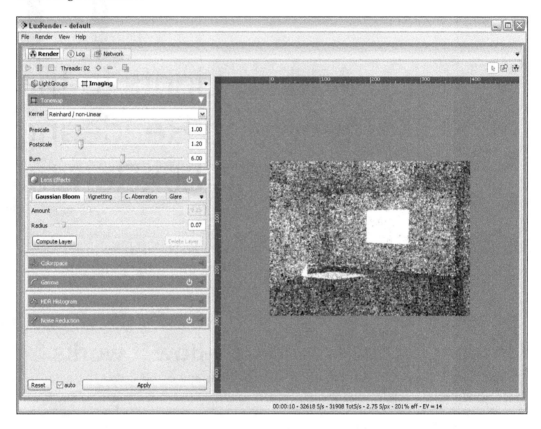

This is just the first interaction of the renderer with the scene, and that's the reason we are seeing a low quality image. With time, the renderer will add more iterations and the image will lose the noise, becoming much clearer. The reason the render method is called a progressive refinement by some artists is that the image is rendered in various steps until we get a final result.

Another interesting point about unbiased render engines is that the number of interactions required to create each image is theoretically infinite. Does that mean that the render could last forever? Yes, in theory, a render created with an unbiased render engine could refine the image forever.

One of the tricks when working with such render engines is to know the best time to stop the interaction. Each scene and project will have a different render time and number of iterations based on the complexity and objectives of the render. To help the render process, almost all unbiased render engines allow us to do a few tricks with the render progress:

- At any moment, we can pause the render and resume later
- Each core of your CPU can take care of one iteration, which will boost up the render progression
- A few adjustments to the scene can be made to avoid the loss of interactions while the render is in progress

How to add light sources in LuxRender

First, we will set up all of the required light sources in LuxRender. Because LuxRender works with the physical behavior of light, we can't use the default light sources of Blender 3D. These lights are mostly based on single points that emit light energy, which doesn't occur in the real world. For LuxRender, we have to use objects that emit light energy based on the material assigned in LuxBlend.

Just like we saw in the LuxBlend materials settings in the last chapter, we have a material type called **Light**. Every time an object has a light material type assigned, it will work as a light source.

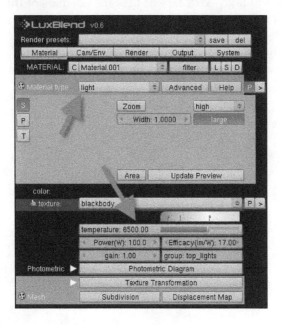

When we choose the light material, a parameter will be available to set up how the light will behave:

- **Temperature**: With this option, we can choose the light temperature, which will determine the color of the light as well. In LuxBlend, we have a scale of colors to aid in the selection of the best temperature. All temperatures are in the Kelvin scale. For instance, the sunlight has a temperature of about 5500K and a studio lamp has one of about 3400K.

- **Power (W)**: Here, we can control the power of the light in Watts.

- **Efficacy (lm/W)**: The efficacy of the light is determined here by using a scale of Lumens/Watts. The sunlight has an efficacy of about 93 lm/w, and a fluorescent light can start with an efficacy of 15 and go up to 35.

- **Gain**: This is a multiplier value that controls all settings of the light source.

- **Group**: Here, we can name a light group to control the light source. We will learn more about light groups later in this chapter.

Using objects as light sources

Now that we know that the best option to use lights in LuxRender is by using objects to emit light, we will add some of them to the scene. The objective here is to create a mesh plane and make it work as an area light. Add a mesh plane to the scene, and assign a material to the object called **light_ceiling**. When using an object like a plane to emit light, we have to take extra care of the face normals of the plane or 3D mesh because the normals will determine the direction of the emission of light.

Select the object and make sure that the normals are pointing down, like the following image shows:

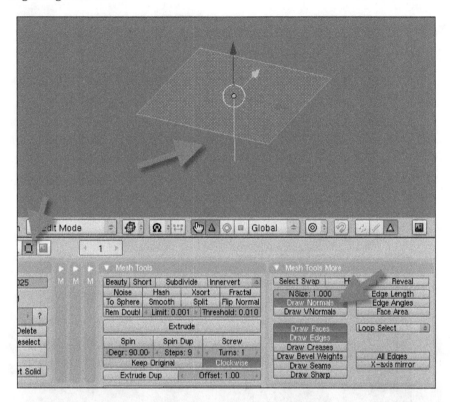

The controls to display face normals are located in the mesh editing panel on the right. To flip a face normal, we can select the face in edit mode, press the *W* key, and choose **Flip Normals**.

With the plane created, create several instances of the plane with the *Alt+D* keys, and organize them like the following image shows:

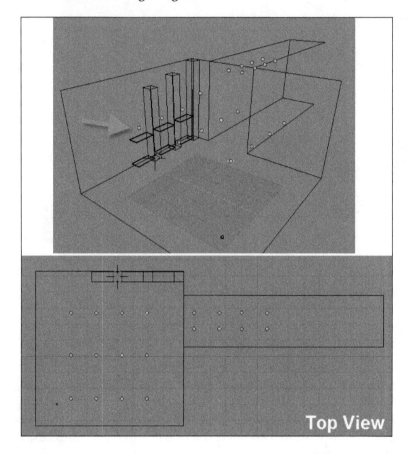

We can also use the array modifier to distribute the planes on the scene.

In LuxBlend, we will set up the material as a light type and assign a color of 6500K and a multiplier of 1. The other parameters will stay with the default values.

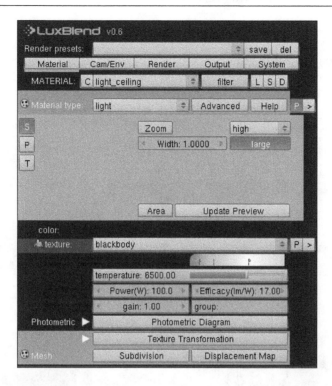

Light groups

To complete the setup of the mesh plane as light sources, we have to create a light group to control the lights later, while the image is rendering. When we have a scene with several light sources, we can group them by name and change the settings of those lights while the image is still rendering. This is one of the best features of LuxRender, and it will enable us to create animations with lights and generate various images with different settings for all lights.

With the plane still selected, add the name **top_lights** in the **group:** field of the light material.

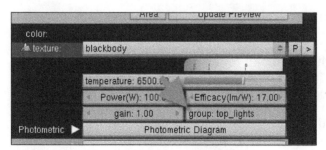

With the planes already placed and distributed around the scenario, we can work on the other light sources of the project, which are the small lamps that we created in Chapter 12, *Using Modifiers and Curves to Create Details for the Robot and Scene*. Select the center of the object, and add a material called **Light_ground**. This will also be a light type, so set it to be in a light group called **ground**.

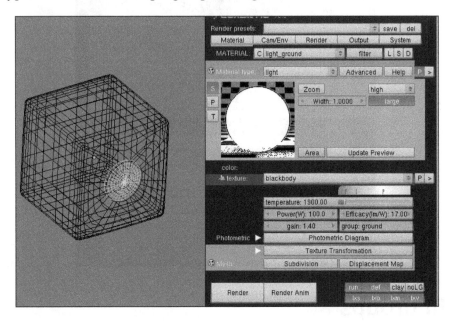

The temperature should be 1900K, and the gain will be 1.4.

Now, select all the small lamp models and press *Shift+D* to duplicate the object without any link to the original object. Select only the small area that will represent the light emitter, and add another material to it called **wall_lights**. Set it as a light material and repeat the same settings of the previous one, changing only the light group name to **walls**.

This will give us three different light groups to work with:

- Ground
- Walls
- Top_lights

What can we do with these groups? While the image is rendering, we will be able to turn all lights in those groups on and off, as well as change some parameters such as temperature and gain.

Before we hit **Render**, let's distribute the lights around the set. Select the small light source we just created (the one with the **wall_lights** material). Create several copies with the *Alt+D* keys to create linked copies, and place them as shown in the following image:

Notice the small light box dropped on the ground. It's also a light source. Set your camera to look at the scene at an angle similar to the one in the previous image. One last step required before we hit render is the environment setup. In LuxRender, we must set how the environment will be used during rendering.

Environment for rendering

To change the environment used in the rendering, go to the **Cam/Env** tab to choose from several options related to the environment. Mostly in LuxRender, we'll choose either SunSky or none. The SunSky environment uses a sun lamp to simulate the sun, and with only artificial light sources like the ones we use in the project, we have to choose none. This will only add light energy to the scene based on objects with light materials.

Go to the **Cam/Env** tab and choose **none** as the environment.

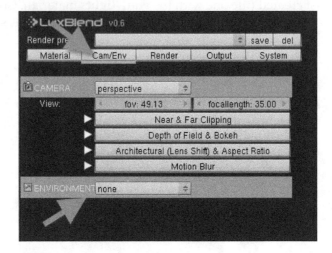

Rendering the scene

It's time to render the scene and see what all those lights added to the scenario will look like in LuxRender. To add a bit more detail to the scene, place five copies of the box created in Chapter 12 *Using Modifiers and Curves to Create Details for the Robot and Scene* to populate the set. The composition should look like the following image:

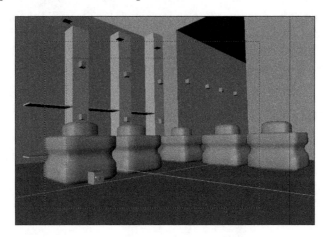

Hit the **Render** button and we will see the LuxRender renderer popping up, and the scene will be loaded. You will see a very grainy image that becomes clearer as time passes. In a few minutes, we will see a screenshot like the following:

Notice on the left that we have a few controls for light groups identified by the names we gave in LuxBlend.

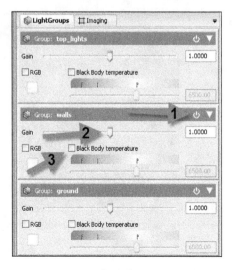

Each light group has three main controls:

1. Button to turn on and off
2. Gain slider
3. Light temperature enabling or disabling option

For instance, let's see what will happen if we turn off the **walls** group.

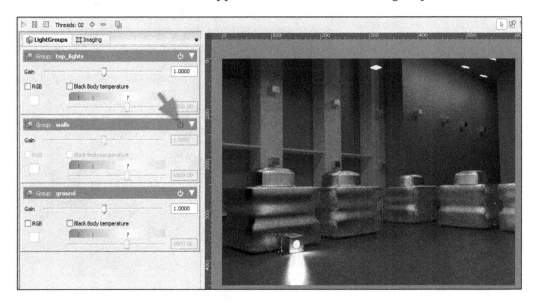

With the **walls** group turned on again, we will now increase the **Gain** of the group.

All these changes are visible during the render and can be adjusted while the image is refining. To create different versions of the same rendering, all we have to do is copy the image with the changes using the button located in the upper part of the interface.

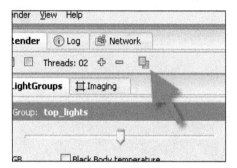

Open GIMP or any image editor and paste the image there. With lots of changes in the rendering process, we can create a number of versions for the same project.

Summary

This chapter was about setting up lights in LuxRender to create realistic images with very few adjustments or edits. Besides the setup of LuxRender, we also added lots of elements and created the scenario to receive the robot model in preparation for the next chapter.

Here is a list of things that we have learned:

- What an unbiased render engine is and how it works
- How to set up lights to work with LuxRender
- How to set up objects to emit light
- What light groups are
- How to edit light groups
- How to choose the environment in LuxRender
- How to render with LuxRender

15
It's Alive! Animating the Robot

In this chapter, we will assemble our robot and use animation tools to create the transforming movement of the machine. By using the same controls, we can easily create animations with Blender and render the movement in LuxRender. After this chapter, we will be able to pose the robot in any way that we like in order to create different scenes and compositions with lots of characters.

Animation controls and hierarchies

All of the parts and pieces of the robot were created as separated objects. If we try to move them around now, the result of the movement won't affect other objects. To fix that and make the robot behave like a single object while still enabling the creation of animations and movements in parts such as arms, legs, and joints), we have to set up a hierarchy. In 3D animation software, it's also called *parenting* an object to another. For instance, we can make the foot of an object to be parented to the leg.

In this case, the foot will be a child object in relation to the leg, and every time the leg moves or rotates, the foot will follow the same transformations. However, when the foot is transformed around, the leg won't suffer any transformations.

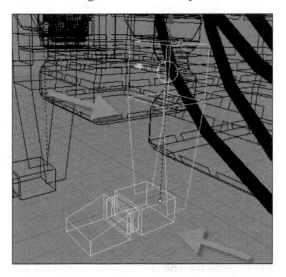

To parent objects in Blender 3D, we must select the objects and press the *Ctrl+P* keys. The selection order is quite important in the parenting setup, and we must always leave the child objects first. For instance, to set up the hierarchy between the foot and leg, the foot must be selected first.

Removing the hierarchy

To remove the parenting relation between two objects, select the child object and press the *Alt+P* keys. This will call a tool named **Clear Parent**. It's an important option that is useful when something goes wrong with the parenting setup.

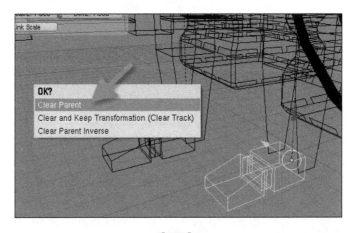

Joints and pivots

The setup of the robot won't be complete without the correct placement of joints to create articulated areas between parts of the robot. To create a joint, we'll deal with helper objects placed between 3D models. The objective of those helpers is to add control over the pivot points for animation, without the need to change the center point of those objects. For instance, if we select any part of the robot's arm and try to rotate it, the result will be a rotation taking place from the center point of the 3D model. This is its pivot point.

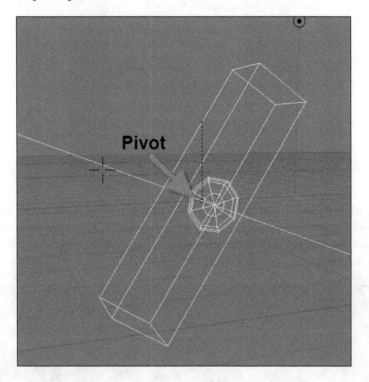

To change this pivot point, we have two options—the setup of the center point on the sides of the 3D model or the addition of a helper object.

Using empties as helper objects

In Blender, we have an object called an **Empty**, which is mostly used as a helper for animation tasks. As the name says, the object has no geometry nor does it show up in render. It only works as a way to add controllers or new pivots to objects. To create a new **Empty**, we can choose the object type in the toolbox.

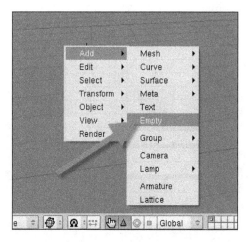

The visualization of an empty object is quite simple, and in most of the cases, we will only need the point representation. To change the way an empty looks in the 3D view, open the **Object** panel and choose to display the bounds of the empty or the name to help with the visualization.

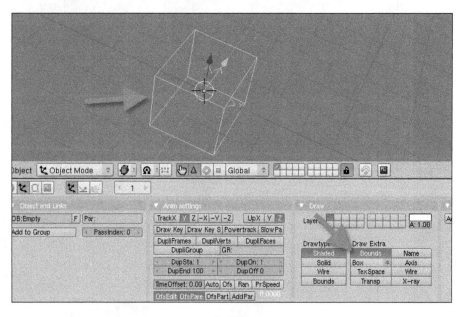

To use an empty as a pivot point, we have to add the object between two parts of a hierarchy. For instance, an empty could be placed as the shoulder of the robot.

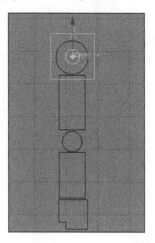

After setting up the parenting between objects, we will be able to rotate the empty and use it as the shoulder. This same setup can be repeated for all other parts of the robot.

Pivots without empties

Another way to set up pivot points without the need of empties is with the objects' centers. All of the objects in Blender 3D use their center points as pivots, and those points are located at the bounding box center of the object. We can change the position of the center point and make the object rotate using any part of the model. To change the center point, use the 3D cursor and the snap tool. Select any vertex of the object and, using the *Shift+S* keys, align the cursor to the selection.

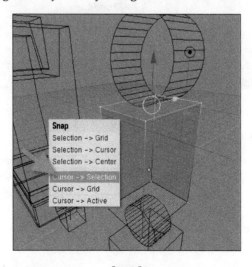

While in object mode, go to the editing panel and press the **Center Cursor** button. The object's center will be placed at the position of the 3D cursor.

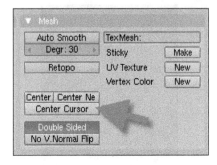

If we try to rotate the object now, it will use the center point as a pivot. If you want to use other options as pivots, you can find the pivot selector at the header of the 3D view (2).

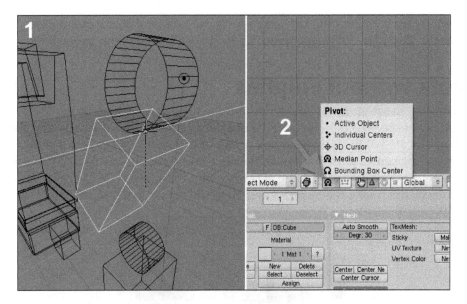

Posing the robot

Now that we know how to create pivots with and without empties, it's time to set up the joints of the robot. The process of adding pivot points to the robot will allow us to easily create a retracted form of the robot and a humanoid shape. The following image shows the robot in both forms. With that in mind, we will set up the pivots to move all parts of the robot in order to create and change shapes easily.

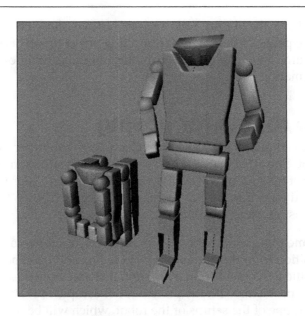

Before anything else, we have to duplicate all parts of the robot and create its humanoid shape. The humanoid shape of the robot will be easier to set up and more familiar to add the required joints and place pivots.

To create the setup for the robot, we will add empties along the identified positions where we should have a joint. Those places are marked in the following image:

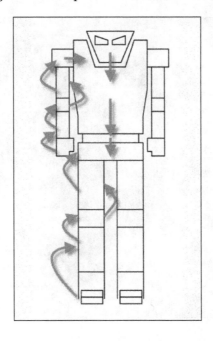

Set up the hierarchy of the objects, following the arrows shown in the last image. This will make the pelvis of the robot a controlling object for all of the objects in the hierarchy. Every time we move or transform this object, all other objects will follow the same transformation.

Using two robots for posing

A common trick in animations is to use two characters with different setups for each type of movement. The artist uses the best setup for each situation of the acting. For instance, we can set up a robot with joints and pivots for an easier transformation from the humanoid form into the box form, and vice versa. When the movement is completed, the artist replaces the model.

We can do the same thing for the robot animation—creating two different setups to make the transition from the humanoid form to box and from box to humanoid. The dynamics of the movement from a humanoid character makes this approach useful in avoiding problems with the placement of complex pivots. In the last section, we created one of the setups of the robot, which will be used to animate the model in humanoid form. Now, it's time to create the pivots and joints to set up the transformation.

In the copied object, without any empties or hierarchies, we will rotate and add the joints of the object in order to create a box shape, like the one shown in the following image:

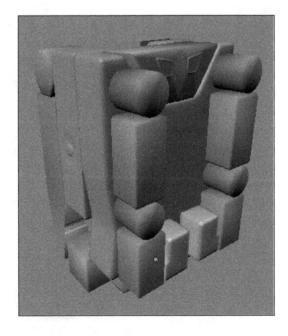

To help with the visualization of the transformation and the best placement of the joints, refer to the next image, which shows all pieces with a fifty percent transformation:

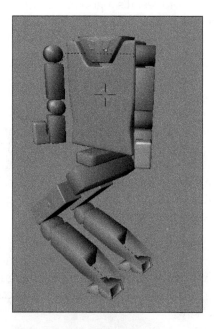

All of the transformations suffered by single objects will be based on rotations. Add empties to create joints at the positions identified in the following diagram:

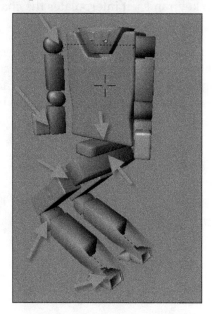

With the empties placed, it will be easy to rotate and create intermediate poses between both states of the robot.

Even with the model having empties, it's a good strategy to have a simple boxed robot to use in scenes or shots where the object won't suffer any movements. This will be important for our project, especially in the next section when we will distribute the robot along the scene.

Basic animation with the robot

With the character ready to be animated, it's time to add some movements to the robot. Animation is a complex and huge subject and would be better explained in a book dedicated exclusively to animation. But it doesn't mean that we can't explore some basic concepts and tools to create movement for the robot. The final animation of this project will be created in LuxRender by using light groups, but it could use some movements on the robot to extend the project.

An animation is nothing more than a series of still images played in a sequence. If the speed of the played images reaches a certain speed, your brain starts to view the image as an animation. This limit is approximately 24 images per second. In Blender, each still image from an animation is called a frame. How can we create this series of images to create an animation?

There is a special type of frame called keyframe, which can mark a change in the position of any property of an object. When the animation software finds a difference in a property between two keyframes, it interpolates the change automatically to create movement.

For instance, let us consider that we have a keyframe in frame 1 where an object has a rotation of zero degrees in the X axis, and another keyframe in frame 60 with a rotation set to 90 degrees in the same axis. When we hit play, the 3D animation software will create the intermediate positions to represent the rotation as movement.

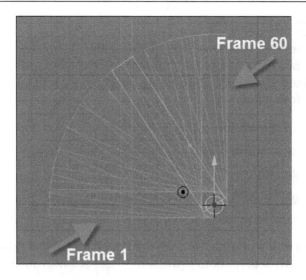

Adding keyframes and movement

To manage the animation and add keyframes to the object, we can work with the timeline window in Blender. Add a new horizontal division to the interface, and create a **Timeline** window. This window has several animation controls such as play, rewind, forward, record keyframe, and so on.

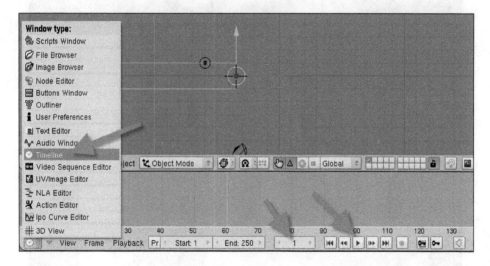

Besides the basic controls, we will find the start and end frame of an animation created in Blender.

Animating objects

We can add keyframes in the 3D view by pressing the *I* key when the desired frame is selected. For instance, we can move or rotate an object and move the playback head of the timeline to frame 20. By pressing the *I* key, we will be able to add keyframes for the following:

- **Loc**: Only for translation
- **Rot**: Only for rotation
- **Size**: Only for scale
- **LocRot**: Keys for both translation and rotation
- **LocRotSize**: Keys for translation, rotation, and scale

For our project, we will work mainly with the translation and rotation of objects. The concept of working with them both is the same. Let's see how to animate an arm of the robot.

First, we select only the arm and add a rotation keyframe by setting the frame to **1** and by pressing the *I* key when the mouse cursor is in the 3D view. Choose **Rot** as the keyframe type.

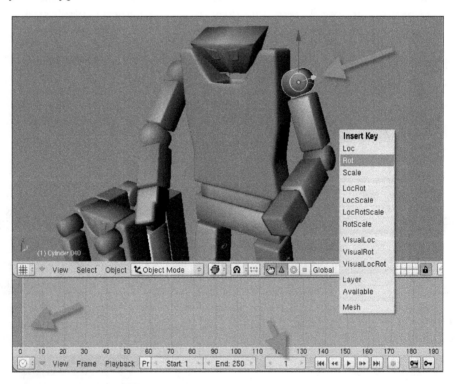

Now, change the frame to **30** and rotate the arm just a bit. If you want to use precision in the rotation, press the *N* key and add the rotation to the Y axis in the **Properties** panel, or hold the *Ctrl* key and rotate the object with the *R* key. For this example, we can use 30 degrees in the Y axis. When the object is rotated, press the *I* key and create a new keyframe for **Rot**.

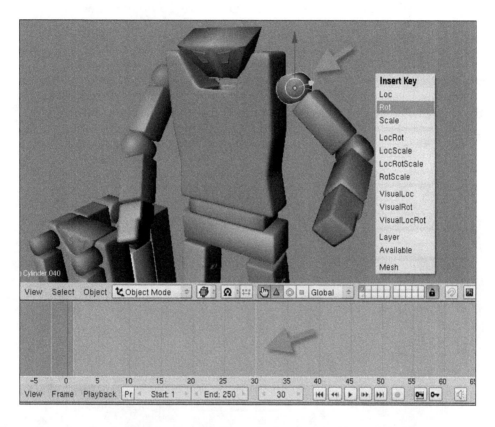

If we press the play button in the timeline window, we will see the object rotation between frames 1 and 30.

To speed up the animation process, we can use the record button in the timeline, which automatically adds keyframes to the selected objects. Here is how it works:

1. Turn the record key, and choose the **Add/Replace** keys from the drop-down menu right next to the button.

2. Set the frame at the start of the animation.

3. Select the object and place it in the initial position of the animation.

4. Move the playback head to the next frame where a keyframe should be added.

5. Transform the object by moving, rotating, or scaling.

6. Turn off the record button.

If we press the play button, all keyframes will be added automatically.

Erasing keyframes

There are several ways to erase a keyframe if we added one by mistake in the wrong frame. To erase keyframes with the timeline window, use the small key icon on the window header, or press the *Alt+I* keys. Place the playback head over the frame where the keyframe is placed, and click once on the icon. Choose the type of keyframe that must be erased, and it will be removed from the timeline.

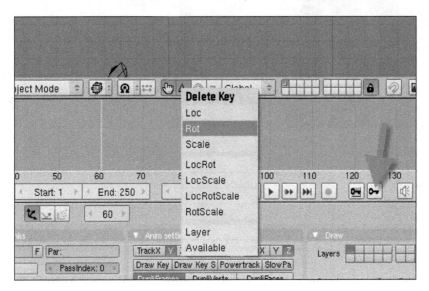

To do that, an object must be selected in the 3D view.

Distributing the robots

The next step is to distribute the objects around the scene. As our rendering in LuxRender deals with light groups rather than animated objects, the process of populating the scene with objects will use the box shape of the robot and the humanoid form. Using the box-shaped robot, we will distribute the object in the positions shown in the following image:

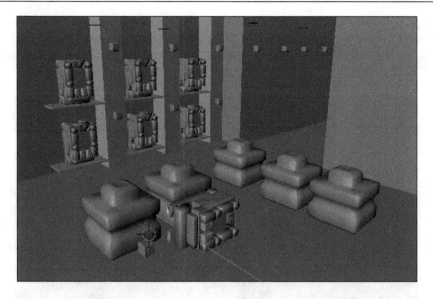

Add a humanoid form robot, and pose it as shown in the following image:

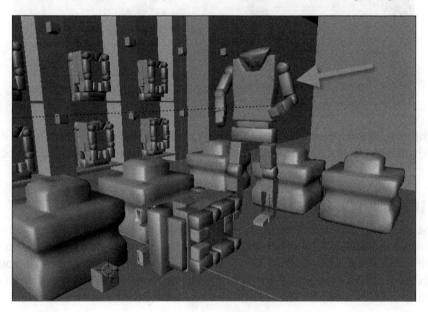

The image will show a few cables attached to the back of the robot, which we created in Chapter 13, *Making the Robot Look Metallic with Materials in LuxRender*. Add those cables to the back of the robot, using a metal material for them, and set the material to look like aluminum.

The light groups are already assigned to the materials that we created in LuxBlend, and with all objects placed in the scene, we can now start rendering our project.

Rendering and animating the lights

With the objects placed in the scene, we can open LuxBlend again and start the rendering of the robots. The process will be exactly the same as the last chapter with the scene alone. However, more light energy will be added to the environment through the lights in eyes and the legs of the robot. Open LuxBlend, and with the same setup that we used for the scene, start rendering the completed scene.

If we turn the controls for the light groups on and off, we will be able to see the image change in real time.

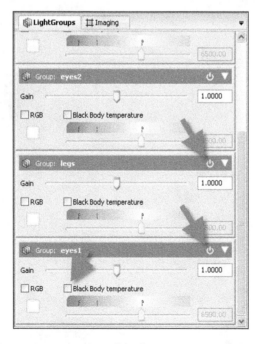

Change the gain value and the **Black Body temperature** to increase the power of all lights on the scene or to change the color of the light.

Summary

In this chapter, we learned how to set up a mechanical animation to the robot model and render it with LuxRender. We had to learn some new concepts and use tools for organic and mechanical animations.

Here is a brief summary of the topics that we have covered in this last chapter:

- The differences between organic and mechanical animation
- How Blender constraints work
- How to use constraints in animation
- What hierarchies are
- How hierarchies work in Blender
- How to set up the hierarchy of the robot
- How to animate constraints
- How to render an animation in LuxRender
- How to assemble a sequence of image files in Blender in order to create a video

16
Post Production of the Robot

In this last chapter of the book and of the robot project, we will take look at the post-production process in LuxRender. In other projects, the normal workflow for adjustments after the rendering would be aimed at some image editor such as GIMP. However, with LuxRender, we have another way to edit and fine-tune the image without the need of image editor software. In this chapter, we will learn how to make the necessary adjustments to the image inside LuxRender.

Using LuxRender for post production

One of the great things about LuxRender is the incredible realism that we can achieve by just changing a few settings in Blender 3D. Sometimes, however, an image needs small changes in brightness, color, or lens effects, which would make the overall scene more realistic. If the renderer is made in a software like YafaRay, the best option to change these settings would be an image editor or even the use of composite nodes in Blender 3D. With LuxRender, these two options could be a problem because it would require the image to be rendered all over again when something needs to be changed.

To solve this problem in LuxRender, we have a side pane that allows us to change several options to increase the realism of an image on the fly. Any changes made to the image are immediately displayed in the render window.

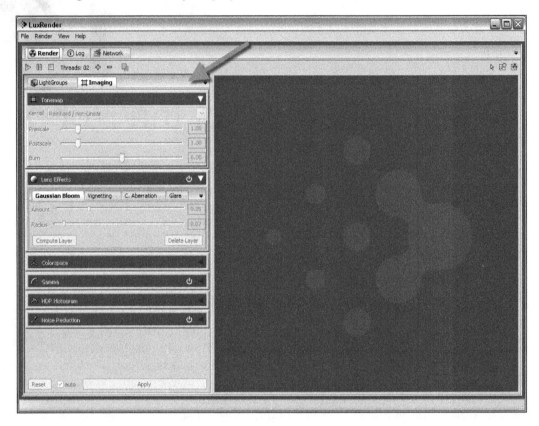

These are the panels available at the side pane in LuxRender:

- **Tonemap**: Here we have options to make adjustments on the light-scale of the scene both on the pre- and post- creation of the image.

- **Lens Effects**: Some lens effects can add a great level of realism to almost all of the scenes. Here, it's possible to add effects such as Vignetting, Gaussian Bloom, and Glare.

- **Colorspace**: With the settings available in this area, we can change the color of the rendered image based on values of red, green, and blue.

- **Gamma**: In this area, it's possible to apply some level of Gamma correction to the images, which will change the brightness of the render.

- **HDR Histogram**: In this field, we can adjust the HDR histogram to change the overall color of the rendered image.

- **Noise Reduction**: In LuxRender, we have a render that occurs in a process called **progressive refinement**. In the earlier stages of the render, the image has a lot of noise and, with these settings, we can remove some of the noise.

All of the settings available in those options can create and change the look and feel of the image while the rendering is still happening. That's the reason for choosing those options instead of relying on image editor software; we can change the image while everything is in refinement.

Even if the render was stopped before, there is an easy way to pause and resume the rendering later.

Saving and resuming a render

It's very important to save the rendering of a scene, even if you don't plan to make changes later, because we will be able to bypass all the initial refinement processes and even change the light settings with light groups. We can even consider this as a rule for our big projects in LuxRender: *always save the project file*.

To save a project file, open the **File** menu in LuxRender when the project has been rendered.

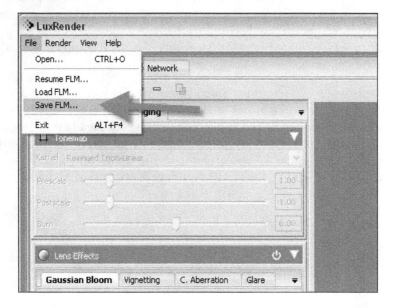

It the menu, we will save two files: one in the FLM file format (that is, the overall scene file), and the other will store the actual progress of the rendering. It's quite important to save the project file several times along the rendering process. If anything goes wrong, such as a computer crash or power problem, all the time spent in the refinement of the image won't be lost.

When the project is saved, we can resume the render by opening the same **File** menu and choosing resume. The software will ask for the project files, which should be saved in a separate folder. If everything is set correctly and the texture files are placed in the same folders, the image will start refining again in a few seconds depending on the image resolution and project size.

Saving the project

Saving the project file can be decisive to a rendering because we will be able to make changes inside LuxRender rather than in an image editor. All changes made inside the LuxRender editor are far better than anything arranged in software like GIMP or Photoshop.

Applying lens effects

In the **Lens Effects** area, we can add several lens effects directly to the rendered image and see the results almost in real time. Depending on the complexity of the scene and the available resources for your computer, it may take a few moments for the rendered scene to get updated with the effects. All the effects that are grouped in the lens effects area are related to real distortions of optical events that really occur in photography and cinema.

Choosing those effects will result in some interesting changes in the image, which will make our render look like a shot taken by a photographer. We only have to take care of the amount of effects added to a single image because even in LuxRender, these effects can take a long time to compute and slow down the refinement process. In some cases, it may even be the reason for a crash on the computer. It's a good practice to save the project every time a lens effect is applied to avoid any loss of data.

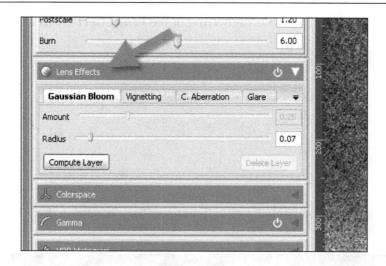

Gaussian Bloom

Gaussian Bloom is a filter we use to add a bit of glow to the lights in the scene, similar to a lens effect. The difference here is that, with this effect, we will add a mix of blur and glow instead of rays derived from a lens distortion. But, the result will be a very bright spot of light in our scene. As this effect is applied directly on the light sources, the best results will occur when we use the effect in a scene with a visible light source.

We can enable the effect by checking the option shown in the following screenshot:

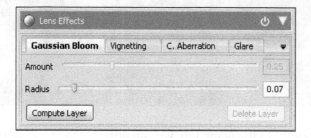

Vignetting

The Vignetting effect is a common optical effect associated with old photograph machines, where a dark border appears around the image. With an effect like this, we can simulate the look of an old photograph and make the rendered image even more realistic, especially if the image has something to do with a steampunk environment. This is not the case for the robot project, but with a few tweaks it could really improve the overall result of the render.

To use this effect, simply enable **Vignetting** in the **Lens Effect** tab as follows:

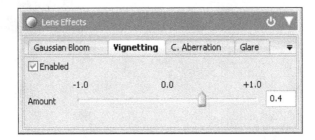

Right after the option is enabled, you will notice a dark border in the rendering window.

With the slider located in the same tab, we can either increase or decrease the size of the dark border.

C. Aberration

A Chromatic Aberration is a common effect associated with not-so-sophisticated lenses, which can create fringes from the different colors of the spectrum. This is an effect that doesn't appear in professional cameras, but in can make the rendered image look like a photo taken by a regular camera. With this effect, we will see some fringes of lights around the focused light source.

If we want to use this effect, all we have to do is turn the **C. Aberration** option on, which is available in the **Lens Effects** panel:

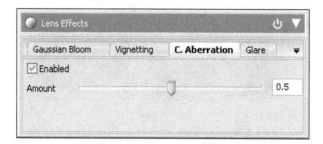

There are options to set the amount of aberration that we want to see in the rendered image. It's quite important to focus on the light source to create this type of effect on the images.

Glare

The Glare effect is one of the most famous and common effects applied to an image seen through a lens. With this effect, we can create that flare of light coming out of an image (which is very common in images) that focuses a strong light source like the sun. To create this effect in the scene, we have to set the amount of glare that we want and the number of Blades generated by the glare. To generate the glare effect, aim the camera focus directly at some source of light.

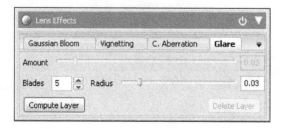

HDR Histogram

A histogram is used more for analysis than for making changes or adjustments to the image. With this tool, we can get a good view of the distribution of pixels along the color spectrum. It's a tool with significant use in photography and is available in most photo-editing software like Photoshop, Lightroom, and Aperture. We can use this tool to get a view of the distribution of the pixels right after making some changes to the brightness of the render or colors.

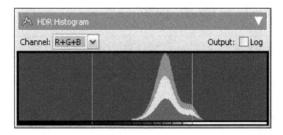

It's not difficult to find uses for a histogram view after changes to the image. For instance, if we make an image that is a representation of a daylight scene, a good number of pixels should be placed in the white areas of the spectrum. A night scene, or even a studio render, will show a graph where a good number of pixels is placed near the black color.

Noise reduction

The best way to remove the noise of the rendered images in LuxRender is to let the refinement run long enough to remove all artifacts from the image. But, there are some projects that require an image to be rendered quickly and can't afford to wait for the render to remove all the noise. With an option called **Noise Reduction**, we can find a way to filter the noise of an image using a mixture of effects, such as blur, to remove the graininess from the entire image.

This tool won't make the render process any faster, but it can help to create render tests of projects before it's left to render for more time.

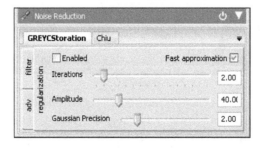

To remove the noise, several different adjustments will be necessary depending on that particular project. Knowing each option and parameter well is not enough; we will still have to make changes on the fly to find the best settings for each project.

Select the **Enabled** checkbox, and tweak the filter with the **Iterations**, **Gaussian Precision**, and **Amplitude** settings.

The final result after using the noise reduction tool will be very similar to a Gaussian blur filter available in GIMP or Photoshop. With a few tweaks, it's possible to get a good-looking filter for the rendered image. Still, it can take some time until you find the best settings.

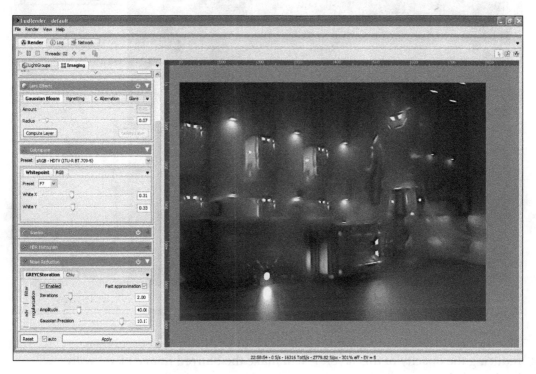

Removing the noise in GIMP

A good workaround to get the noise removed from the image is to use a combination of filters in GIMP. In this case, it will be faster to edit the rendered image outside of LuxRender. The trick is quite simple and requires only a small addition in GIMP. Open the rendered image, and in the **Layers** panel, create a copy of the layer where the image is placed.

The trick consists of adding some Gaussian blur to the top layer and then reducing the opacity of this layer. It will make the blurred image blend with the layer below.

As a result, we will have an image with a slight glow effect, but without most of the noise from the image.

Summary

In this last chapter, we learned more about the post production options in LuxRender, which can be executed at the renderer window. Another great aspect of LuxRender is that we don't need an image editor to make adjustments to the renderer image because the time spent on the refinement process is too long.

We have learned how to do the following:

- Post production of rendered images in LuxRender
- Add lens effects in the rendering to make the image look like a photograph
- Add color schemes to fit artificial and natural lighting
- Remove the noise of the image with LuxRender
- Remove the noise of the image with GIMP

Index

K

keyframe, basic animation
  about 272
  adding 273
  erasing 276
keys
  0 key 35
  B key 32
  Ctrl+Alt+0 key 95
  Ctrl+H key 50
  Ctrl+M key 121, 122
  Ctrl+N key 59
  Ctrl+P key 225
  Ctrl+R key 31, 33, 62
  Ctrl+Shift+N key 59
  Ctrl+Space 29
  Ctrl+Tab 29
  Ctrl+Tab key 30
  Ctrl+Z 30
  Ctrl key 85
  E key 29
  Esc key 29
  F5 key 88
  G key 34
  I key 274
  M key 234
  P key 85, 246
  Shift+D key 66, 89
  Shift+S key 51
  S key 35
  T key 149
  W key 73
  Y key 35
  Z key 84

L

lens effects
  applying 284
  C. Aberration effect 287
  Gaussian Bloom 285
  HDR Histogram 288
  Vignetting effect 285, 286
light sources
  adding, in LuxRender 251-257
  animating 279, 280

Array Modifier, using 254
  light group, creating 255, 256
  light group, types 256, 257
  light group, using 256
  light material, parameters 252
  modeling, steps 235
  objects, using 252-255
  rendering 279, 280
  rendering environment, modifying 257, 258
  types 235
Live Unwrap Transform tool 167, 168
LuxBlend
  .lxm file 241
  .lxo file 241
  .lxs file 241
  .lxv file 241
  about 239
  Cam/Env tab 240
  Clay button 240
  controls 240
  Def button 240
  image 240
  materials, adding to light model 244-246
  materials, loading 243, 244
  materials, setting up 241, 242
  materials, types 242
  material tab 240
  noLG button 240
  output tab 240
  rendering process 240
  Render tab 240
  Run button 240
  system tab 240
  using 239-241
LuxRender
  downloading 237
  installing 237-239
  light sources, adding 251
  LuxBlend, using 239-241
  noise, reducing 288, 289
  problems, solving 282
  rendering 207
  scene rendering, resuming 283, 284
  scene rendering, saving 283, 284
  side pane, panels 282, 283
  using, for post-production 281

M

main body
  modeling 214
materials, YafaRay
  cockpit glass, setting 198, 199
  metal material, setting 198
  working on 197
M key
  using 234
model, detailing
  poly modeling used 57
modeling
  mixing, with animation 207
  objects, poly modeling used 208
  technique, choosing 209
modeling technique
  choosing 209-212
  legs, modeling 210, 211
  poly modeling 209
  subdivision modeling 209
modifiers
  about 219, 220
  array 219, 223
  bevel 219, 220
  mesh deform 220
  simple deform 220

N

NaN company 9
night simulations
  rendering 200, 201
Not a Number. *See* **NaN company**

O

objects
  animating 274, 275
  modeling 30
  using 252-255
objects tab, YafaRay 91
output tab 240

P

particle system
  actual setup 178-180

  adding, to rear engine 184
  basic element parameters, settings 179
  creating, in Blender 176, 177
  emitter 177
  force fields, adding 181
  hair 177
  interaction parameter 178
  life parameter 177
  mesh emitting parameter 177
  motion parameter 178
  physics parameter 178
  quantity parameter 177
  reactor 177
  speed fields, adding 181-183
  visualization parameter 178
  working 177
PBX 12
physical sky setup
  DarkTide's SunSky background 195, 196
  gradient type 193
  single color, choosing 192
  steps 192
  Sunsky background 194-196
  texture, adding 193, 194
  texture, HRDI used 193
  YafaRay, using 191
pivot
  about 265
  Empty, not using 267, 268
  Empty, using as helper objects 266, 267
  point, changing 266
P key 246
polygon modeling, of weapon
  about 23
  background image, adding 24, 25
  extrusion, creating 28, 30
  final touches 53-55
  keyboard shortcuts 28
  object, modeling 30
polygon modeling, subdivision used
  Blender, work modes 26
  cube, creating 26
  cube, modifying 27
  hand wrap, modeling 38-44
  sequential extrusions set, creating 32, 33
  small parts, modeling 45

Packt Open Source Project Royalties

When we sell a book written on an Open Source project, we pay a royalty directly to that project. Therefore by purchasing Blender 3D 2.49 Incredible Machines, Packt will have given some of the money received to the Blender project.

In the long term, we see ourselves and you — customers and readers of our books — as part of the Open Source ecosystem, providing sustainable revenue for the projects we publish on. Our aim at Packt is to establish publishing royalties as an essential part of the service and support a business model that sustains Open Source.

If you're working with an Open Source project that you would like us to publish on, and subsequently pay royalties to, please get in touch with us.

Writing for Packt

We welcome all inquiries from people who are interested in authoring. Book proposals should be sent to authors@packtpub.com. If your book idea is still at an early stage and you would like to discuss it first before writing a formal book proposal, contact us; one of our commissioning editors will get in touch with you.

We're not just looking for published authors; if you have strong technical skills but no writing experience, our experienced editors can help you develop a writing career, or simply get some additional reward for your expertise.

About Packt Publishing

Packt, pronounced 'packed', published its first book "Mastering phpMyAdmin for Effective MySQL Management" in April 2004 and subsequently continued to specialize in publishing highly focused books on specific technologies and solutions.

Our books and publications share the experiences of your fellow IT professionals in adapting and customizing today's systems, applications, and frameworks. Our solution-based books give you the knowledge and power to customize the software and technologies you're using to get the job done. Packt books are more specific and less general than the IT books you have seen in the past. Our unique business model allows us to bring you more focused information, giving you more of what you need to know, and less of what you don't.

Packt is a modern, yet unique publishing company, which focuses on producing quality, cutting-edge books for communities of developers, administrators, and newbies alike. For more information, please visit our website: www.PacktPub.com.

Blender 3D: Architecture, Buildings, and Scenery

ISBN: 978-1-847193-67-4   Paperback: 332 pages

Create photorealistic 3D architectural visualizations of buildings, interiors, and environmental scenery

1. Turn your architectural plans into a model

2. Study modeling, materials, textures, and light basics in Blender

3. Create photo-realistic images in detail

4. Create realistic virtual tours of buildings and scenes

Scratch 1.4: Beginner's Guide

ISBN: 978-1-847196-76-7   Paperback: 264 pages

Learn to program while creating interactive stories, games, and multimedia projects using Scratch

1. Create interactive stories, games, and multimedia projects that you can reuse in your own classroom

2. Learn computer programming basics – no computer science degree required

3. Connect with the Scratch community for inspiration, advice, and collaboration

4. Provides hands-on projects that help you learn by experiment and play

Please check **www.PacktPub.com** for information on our titles

Papervision3D Essentials

ISBN: 978-1-847195-72-2   Paperback: 428 pages

Create interactive Papervision 3D applications with stunning effects and powerful animations

1. Build stunning, interactive Papervision3D applications from scratch

2. Export and import 3D models from Autodesk 3ds Max, SketchUp and Blender to Papervision3D

3. In-depth coverage of important 3D concepts with demo applications, screenshots and example code.

4. Step-by-step guide for beginners and professionals with tips and tricks based on the authors' practical

Flash with Drupal

ISBN: 978-1-847197-58-0   Paperback: 380 pages

Build dynamic, content-rich Flash CS3 and CS4 applications for Drupal 6

1. Learn to integrate Flash applications with Drupal CMS

2. Explore a new approach where Flash and HTML components are intermixed to provide a hybrid Flash-Drupal architecture

3. Build a custom audio and video player in Flash and link it to Drupal

4. Build a Flash driven 5-star voting system for Drupal at the end of the book

Please check **www.PacktPub.com** for information on our titles

www.ingramcontent.com/pod-product-compliance
Lightning Source LLC
Chambersburg PA
CBHW062107050326
40690CB00016B/3231